ANSWERING
THE CALL

ANSWERING
THE CALL

HENDRICKSON
PUBLISHERS

Answering the Call: Saving Innocent Lives One Woman at a Time, Updated Edition

© 2012 Hendrickson Publishers Marketing, LLC
P. O. Box 3473
Peabody, Massachusetts 01961-3473

ISBN 978-1-61970-029-1

Printed in the United States of America

Fourth Printing Updated Edition — November 2016

Unless otherwise indicated, Scripture quotations are taken from The Holy Bible, English Standard Version® (ESV®). Copyright © 2001 by Crossway, a publishing ministry of Good News Publishers. All rights reserved.

Scripture quotations marked NIV are taken from the Holy Bible, New International Version®, NIV®. Copyright © 1973, 1978, 1984, 2011 by Biblica, Inc.™ Used by permission of Zondervan. All rights reserved worldwide. www.zondervan.com The "NIV" and "New International Version" are trademarks registered in the United States Patent and Trademark Office by Biblica, Inc.™

All italics that appear within Scripture quotations are the author's emphasis.

Cover image: ©2010 Nada Stankova/ Flickr/ Getty Images

Library of Congress Cataloging-in-Publication Data

Ensor, John M.
    Answering the call : saving innocent lives, one woman at a time / John Ensor. — 2nd ed.
        p. cm.
    Includes bibliographical references.
    ISBN 978-1-61970-029-1 (alk. paper)
    1. Abortion—Religious aspects—Christianity. 2. Pregnancy, Unwanted—Religious aspects—Christianity. 3. Church work with women. 4. Right to life. I. Title.
    HQ766.25.E57 2013
    241'.6976—dc23
                    2012031838

Contents

Preface

The struggle over abortion is now moving into its second generation. Forty years ago, the pro-life movement consisted of a few Catholic voices crying out in the wilderness. Today, hundreds of thousands of Catholic, evangelical, Anglican, and charismatic Christians work side by side in the cause of life all over the world. Along the way, it has won over many others who do not share our Christian faith or worldview. We welcome this. Victory, after all, means that people of every faith or no faith come to understand the injustice of abortion in the same way we have come to see the injustice of slavery. But like the struggle against slavery, the first responders have been Christians motivated by their faith.[1] Even today, it is the Christian faith, and the value of life it places on each individual, that serves as the supply line for the rapidly expanding pro-life movement.

For this reason, I welcome the opportunity to update and revise *Answering the Call*. A second generation must now arise and fill the ranks.

Out of the hard work and generosity of the first generation of the pro-life movement, hundreds of different organizations developed. Some are focused on your neighborhood or county. Others have a statewide, national, or even international mission.

Some pro-life organizations have an educational mission. Some equip students with a pro-life apologetic. Some are dedicated to exposing the violence of abortion itself. Others concentrate on educating the public about biological human development and showcase the beauty of unborn human life. Still others educate the public on the physical and psychological after-effects of abortion. Some are collecting and publishing affidavits from men and women who regret their abortions. Some address the spreading tentacles of utilitarian thinking as it reformulates into physician-assisted suicide, cloning, embryonic stem-cell research, and gendercide.

There are now pro-life organizations that are legislative and political in their mission. Some engage in the democratic process to get pro-life values represented at all levels of government. Some work with legislators to draft just laws and protections that lessen abortion, if not outlaw it altogether. Some work on case law and focus on the courts.

Legal abortion was justified in part as a private matter between a woman and her doctor. So pro-life medical associations have emerged. Some focus on doctors-in-training, helping them resist being forced to train in abortion procedures. Others link arms with pregnancy help medical clinics and serve as medical directors for their ultrasound services.

There are pro-life legal defense organizations. There are pro-life research organizations. There are pro-life clergy associations. There are networks of pro-life writers, bloggers, artists, and musicians. There are teens for life and motorcyclists for life and iPhone-users for life (well, maybe not, but you could start one and even design an app!). This book especially encourages direct, lifesaving intervention through your nearest pregnancy help center. But whatever you do in *answering the call,* do it with all your might and with faith toward God.

Finally, whether you identify with the first or second pro-life generation, think Wilberforce! Whether it's ending the slave trade of his day, or ending the abortion trade today, it will take many of us working together with Wilberforce-like resolve:

> Never, never will we desist till we . . . extinguish every trace of this bloody traffic, of which our posterity, looking back to the history of these enlightened times, will scarce believe that it has been suffered to exist so long a disgrace and dishonor to this country.[2]

—John Ensor

CHAPTER ONE

The Aroma of Life

A few people in King David's time provided such wise assessment of and bold leadership for their generation that it became their lasting testimony. They were the "men of Issachar," and they were described as men "who had understanding of the times, to know what Israel ought to do" (1 Chron. 12:32). Recognizing the vital need for such people in every age, this book aims to help us think through and lead well on a matter of great importance: cherishing and defending innocent human life.

For the past twenty-three years, I have sought to understand and, in turn, help the Christian community understand the times in which we live, specifically at the intersection of biblical ethics and cultural conflict. I have been invited into countless pulpits to address the painful and sensitive issue of abortion. It has been my unwavering hope each time to fashion a powerful, even historic, life-affirming Christian response. I press on because I see no evidence that any other group of people is capable of taking up this burden. Throughout history, right to the present hour, it has been in large part only the Christian community that has cared enough about their neighbors, including the littlest and weakest ones among us, to oppose with courage and compassion the pagan "rights" of abortion, infanticide, exposure, and abandonment.

In the main, pastors and laypeople alike understand that cherishing and defending innocent human life is a moral mandate. It is the law of love. They understand that abortion is an act of violence that kills a baby and damages every mother and father.

As a moral, ethical, and biblical matter, the sanctity of human life is something we uphold as a matter of creed and intellect. But as pastors and Christian leaders, we are reticent about addressing abortion beyond a fleeting condemnation.

My hope in writing *Answering the Call* is to move us past this reticence. The apostle Paul expects our lives as the Church, the people of God, to be so boldly arresting, so surprisingly gracious, so wooingly fragrant, that we are the very aroma of life itself (2 Cor. 2:16). To be that kind of people, we need leaders like the men of Issachar.

When it comes to abortion, for most people the situation is more like dealing with an unseemly smell coming from the basement while attending a family reunion. Something is wrong, but what should one say? First attempts may be glances toward the basement door, followed by a whisper or two privately ("Am I imagining things, or is there a problem here?"). After a while we may get used to it and forget about the matter. Still, if we love our host family and care about their health, we look for a sensitive but honest way to address it. That is the position many Christians are in today. They want to cherish and defend innocent human life, but they want to do it sensitively and rationally. *Answering the Call* is for them.

The need, of course, is not only to inform people of the divine call to hold each life precious but also to inspire God's people to lifesaving and life-changing intervention on behalf of the weak and the innocent. In general, the Christian community is a life-affirming people. If they are provided a practical venue for demonstrating their concern for needy mothers and babies, they will respond enthusiastically.

Therefore I recommend that the call to cherish and defend innocent human life always be coupled with direct intervention with those in pregnancy distress. Every church in every land can and should be starting or partnering with a local pregnancy help ministry. While many other arenas for life-affirming action cry out for attention, this should be first on the list.

There are two reasons I suggest this. First, all abortion is local; it befalls one woman at a time. Frightened mothers who are planning to abort their babies tomorrow are agonizing tonight in homes in our neighborhoods. Second, the Great Commandment calls us to love our neighbors. A woman in an unplanned pregnancy is truly frightened and feels that her very life is ending—not physically, but emotionally and spiritually. Her life as she has projected it appears threatened by the baby. Abortion in her mind is a desperate act to save her own life. This may not be true. But it feels true.

Strange and perverse as their end is, abortionists parrot the same message that Christ offers to those in trouble: "Come to me, all who labor and are heavy laden, and I will give you rest. Take my yoke upon you . . . and you will find rest for your souls" (Matt. 11:28–29). Abortionists promise salvation and rest too. But they require a very different kind of yoke—death and the spiritual death that flows from the bloodguilt of shedding innocent blood.

We have a special duty as the Christian community to refute the false mercy of the abortion industry, especially, and primarily, in our neighborhoods. We know the true Rescuer, the One who gives life and nourishes it. We can say with the Psalmist, "Hope in God" (43:5). We can teach couples who do not see how they can provide for a child to pray for their daily bread, as we ourselves are learning to do. We can break the lie that says that the baby is a death sentence by testifying to how God used our own sin, shame, and fear to turn our lives around and put us on the path of life. We can help them discover God's provision, if we simply act as neighbors loving neighbors, and do the practical things needed to help them through the crisis.

The same Spirit that raised Christ from the dead lives in us who believe. When we get involved, that power emanates from us as the very aroma of life to a young couple grappling with the greatest crisis of their young lives.

Therefore, we, in His name, should be broadcasting in every neighborhood across the land, "Come to me, all you who are weary and burdened (by an unplanned pregnancy). Take my yoke (the way, the truth, and the life I have found in Christ) and learn from me, for Our God is gentle and humble in heart (neither harsh nor condemning) and you will find rest for your souls (I will show you the better way and you will delight in it). For His yoke is easy and His burden is light."

In practice, the best way to bring this winsome invitation to abortion-vulnerable women and couples in our neighborhoods is to partner with local pregnancy help ministries. Day after day, without fanfare or major funding, they provide mothers in pregnancy distress the support they need to prepare for parenting or adoption.

Heartbeat International, which serves as a training and support organization for pregnancy help ministries, currently lists over 5,700 such ministries in their worldwide directory. Most of them are pregnancy help centers and maternity homes, and almost all of them have started in the last forty years—since abortion was discovered as a right somewhere in the US Constitution. They are funded by donations from folks like you and me. They are staffed by lay-counselors, mostly mature Christian women, many of whom know personally the anguish and guilt that attends abortion.

In five minutes, these Christian women are "in." A young woman enters a pregnancy help center, sits down with a complete stranger, and in just a few minutes, she is pouring out the most intimate details of her life. She is explaining, often through tears, why her pregnancy is the biggest crisis of her life. What a place for the gospel to show up in word and deed.

Dr. James Dobson, who currently leads *Family Talk* radio, has long urged the Christian community to establish and support a neighborhood pregnancy help ministry. He says,

> I consider abortion to be the greatest moral evil of our time, because of the worth of those little babies. At the end of the year a crisis pregnancy center can point to a baby boy, born January 12th, a baby girl, born February 22nd—real, live human beings who

were allowed to live, to be brought into the world, to give love and receive love simply because those organizations exist. Crisis pregnancy centers serve the community, by serving mothers-to-be caught in the most traumatic time of their life.[1]

I have helped establish eleven such centers in four major cities over the last twenty years. I can assure you what Dobson says is true. Churches that have answered the call and put neighborly love into lifesaving action by helping mothers in pregnancy crisis are proving to be the aroma of life.

CHAPTER TWO

The Great Test and the Great Work

I n some ways time is very much like a volcano. There are long periods of relative serenity. Then there are rumblings and stirrings that foreshadow, and then give way to truly frightening and cataclysmic times of fiery destruction. The people witnessing these early outbreaks of fire often resist seeing them as warning signs to flee. Instead, they say, "Well, that is the worst of it." They do not act decisively because they have never lived through and cannot imagine the scope of horror that is about to be unleashed.

The powers of evil rely on this psychological craving for normalcy in the face of mass murder and carnage. They use the periods of relative calm to create a moral and spiritual drowsiness that resists seeing events as warning signs of greater evil coming. Of course some courageous voices do sound the alarm. But the Evil One seems to raise up unbalanced and off-putting voices to say the same things with shrill and discrediting hyperbole that neutralize the sobering voices so that the "whole lot" is dismissed. Then evil explodes and sweeps away souls in a torrent of fire and ash.

Sheep and cattle are steadily calmed and spoken to with familiar and reassuring voices till, BLAM!, the slaughter house does what slaughter houses do. So too, the powers of evil use our fondness of the normal, to keep us moseying along down the path to the slaughter.

The Great Test

So it falls to certain generations that they will live in a time when evil rumbles and then convulses into the shedding of innocent blood all around them. Such was the case, for example, in Germany in the 1940s.

Count Helmut Von Moltke, a devout Christian leader of his generation, learned of the growing human rights abuses of the Nazis. In 1941, he wrote, "Certainly more than a thousand people are murdered . . . every day, and another thousand German men are habituated to murder . . . What shall I say when I am asked: And what did you do during this time?"[1] That is the great test.

What is so diabolically evil about abortion is that it quietly, routinely, and, for the most part invisibly, is sweeping away 45 million souls a year worldwide, without raising much of an alarm or disturbing the routine of life around us. And so we face a great test too. Will we, as followers of Christ, and in increasing strength, courageously and resolutely resist the desire to accommodate and normalize mass child-killing and fight for the lives of the innocent? Or will we grow weary of the struggle—gravitate to a more trendy cause, and let slide uncontested postmodernism's blood-lust for unborn human life?

There have always been sober-minded voices calling us to see the unspeakable and pre-eminent evil of abortion. But there have also been a steady number of shrill voices speaking on behalf of the "pro-life movement." They grab attention as if they are saying, "I am pro-life and crazy. Don't you want to be crazy and pro-life like me?"

As a result, in the public mind, the images that are associated with "pro-life" and "pro-life movement" are not as positive as I think they rightly deserve. This saddens me. It is an obstacle to winning the culture. But enduring distorted voices within the movement and slanderously false characterizations from outside it are part of the warfare against evil—part of the test itself.

The year I graduated from high school, 1973, is the year abortion was declared a constitutional right by the US Supreme Court. Within twenty years, approximately 2,300 abortion businesses were profiting richly doing about 1.5 million abortions a year.

Pope John Paul II helped define this contest, calling it a conflict between the "gospel of life" and the "culture of death."[2] Jerry Falwell, Dr. James D. Kennedy, and Chuck Colson are just a few leading evangelicals who came to agree with John Paul II and called upon the evangelical community to get into the fight for life as well.

They are all gone now. If a generation is forty years, then 2013 marks the official torch passing to the next generation. It is the survivor generation. But it is also a generation that has never known anything but legal and accessible abortion.

In addition, this new generation must cope with the general diminution of human life that legal abortion has wrought. Physician-assisted suicide, cloning, embryonic stem-cell research—each has its accompanying lobby of scientists and movie stars trumpeting utopian benefits. Steadily, utilitarian ethics—the notion that some lives can be destroyed (or left to die) to improve the lives of others—is developing into law and policy. An ever-spiraling increase in the cost of health care and an ever-spiraling national debt means that a volcanic pressure is building to see the sick and the elderly pass in a timely, cost-effective way.[3]

The culture of death is gathering strength. Peter Singer, the Ira DeCamp Professor of Bioethics at

Princeton University, advocates extending so-called abortion rights to include newborns, so that parents might be allowed to kill their babies until the child is deemed "sentient," or self-aware.[4] Singer writes, "killing a newborn baby is never equivalent to killing a person, that is, a being who wants to go on living."[5] While not yet a mainstream idea, Singer is not a lone voice. Even as I update this book, Australian academics, Alberto Giubilini and Francesca Minerva, writing in *The Journal of Medical Ethics*, propose changing the term infanticide to "after-birth abortion." They write:

> We argue that, when circumstances occur *after birth* such that they would have justified abortion, what we call *after-birth abortion* should be permissible . . . We propose to call this practice 'after-birth abortion', rather than 'infanticide', to emphasise that the moral status of the individual killed is comparable with that of a fetus (on which "abortions" in the traditional sense are performed) rather than to that of a child. Therefore, we claim that killing a newborn could be ethically permissible in all the circumstances where abortion would be. Such circumstances include cases where the newborn has the potential to have an (at least) acceptable life, but the well-being of the family is at risk.[6]

Their matter-of-fact proposal indicates how reasonable (read: normal or mainstream) they consider their proposal to be. It is a solidly logical extension of abortion-rights rationale. Even though the "after-birth abortion" proposal was met with a firestorm of protest,[7] nonetheless, infanticide is rising as a practice.

"Girl, 16, said to suffocate infant"
"Teen is charged with killing baby at prom"
"Body of baby found in ditch"

These are real newspaper headlines. Baby "drop boxes" have been set up at hospitals and fire stations, and at some pregnancy help centers, as a way of providing an anonymous and safe way for overwrought mothers to find a life-affirming alternative to infanticide, abandonment, or exposure.

The Great Work

But I have hope that this new generation of Christian leaders are also gathering strength. There are young pastors who are speaking with unusual moral clarity and grace.[8] They are young student leaders, bloggers, investigative reporters, researchers, and activists assuming leadership roles and calling this next generation of Christians to answer the call to cherish and defend innocent human life. Their primary challenge is not with those who call themselves pro-choice. It is with those who identify themselves as pro-life.

Yes, abortion advocates are quite happy that so many Christians today identify themselves as pro-life—just as long as they continue to act pro-choice. Passive acceptance of legal abortion, not agreement with legal abortion, is all they need to win.

Jesus used two spiritual leaders in his parable of the Good Samaritan to show this (Luke 10:25–37). The priest and the Levite represent the same kind of leaders who meet me and take great pains to say, "I am pro-life," and "Abortion is terrible" as if that *alone* fulfills the obligations of love.

Jesus illustrates why passive acceptance of death is just as dishonoring to God as actively beating a man and leaving him to die. The priest and the Levite are not described as approving the beating. We might picture them saying, "That is terrible," and "I am definitely against that!" as they scurry to their appointment. The point Jesus is making is that no matter what they believed in an ethical sense (are they thumbs up or down on beating a man to death?) they did not act pro-life. They were passive acceptors of death. Passive acceptance of death is all that is needed for death to run unchecked. That is why being doctrinally or ethically "pro-life" is rather beside the point.

The only true pro-lifer in the parable is the Samaritan. He sees death crouching at the door and rushes in with life-saving and death-defying actions. This is the great work. It is hard work. It is time-consuming, sometimes dangerous, always costly and interrupting work. God is well pleased with it and we will feel His good pleasure as we do it.

The Golden Rule in Matthew 7:12 is the law of love stated another way. We are to respond to the needs of others as we would hope others would respond to our own need. The human heart, when enriched with divine love, creates a life-cherishing, lifesaving, life-changing dynamic of human effort and creativity.

The great test and the great work confronts us all. A young, sweet-voiced sixteen-year-old called my office, which was established to help women in pregnancy distress. A few minutes into telling her story, she said, "If I don't get an abortion, I'm going to kill myself." After a long pause she whispered, "And after I have my abortion, I know I'm going to kill myself." In that moment I understood again the anguish of an unplanned pregnancy. I saw the multidimensional power of death unleashed in abortion. A baby destroyed, a young girl's sense of self torn apart, parents overwrought by their teenager's pregnancy; but what would they say of her suicide?[9]

This young teenager is my neighbor. What does it mean for me to love her as my neighbor? What is the Christian thing to do? What would you have me say and do for her that you think honors God and would make you proud of the Christian testimony presented to her by my words and actions? If I said I could do nothing for her because I had a prayer meeting to get to, what would the law of love compel you to say to me to help me reconsider?

Consider another real example. One couple came to see me with nine of their ten children in tow. The mother was fifteen weeks pregnant. They were Cambodian immigrants. The husband spoke in broken English, "I got laid off from my job. I have nine children to feed! My wife needs an abortion! I cannot afford another child." His wife sat quietly. Her countenance signaled that she was resigned to help her husband but clearly shaken at the thought of doing something contrary to her whole life experience and maternal nature.

What does the law of love require of me in this situation? What should I say to this couple? If I told you that I wished them well and sent them on their way, would you be pleased with me? Not likely. Prayer is certainly called for, but prayer alone is not all that love is capable of accomplishing in this situation.

A graduate student came to me, pregnant by one of her professors. She was finishing her doctorate and preparing to launch her career. It had taken years of work. Her parents had paid tens of thousands of dollars over the years in tuition bills. Now a baby threatened all her plans and hopes. She needed an abortion. This baby threatened her very life—not so much physically, but the life she had envisioned for herself and worked so hard to achieve. This baby was killing her dreams and goals. In that sense, her abortion was an act of self-preservation.

The father of the baby came in with her to make sure she did not waver on "the things we talked about and on what we had decided to do." In private she confessed that in spite of her situation, she was ambivalent about aborting her baby. She was going through with the abortion to please the father and her parents and her friends, all of whom counseled her that this was "not the time to have a baby." The problem was, she understood that she already *had* a baby. The choice now was whether to nurture or destroy her baby. After a brief conversation, she began to turn her mind away from abortion.

Now the father of the baby erupted. He yelled at me, threatened me, yelled at her, and threatened her. I sat there thinking and praying, What should I say to each of them? What is the Christian thing to do? What does the law of love require of me in this situation? How would you have responded?

In one three-month period, the daughters of three local pastors came to our office. They were embarrassed, extremely frightened, somewhat defiant, and in one case hurt and angered because her father had just thrown her out of the house. One woman came in so frightened that she called herself "X" because she was a senior at a local Christian college. She said, "I've lost my salvation. I know what God thinks about abortion." She was about to abort her faith as well as her baby.

Another couple came in, with a background of drugs and alcoholism. He could not read. Neither of them had a job. They told me that they had been living together for ten years. I asked them if they were married and they said yes. But then they explained: They were both married to someone else! Now a baby was on the way. I tried to hide my shock. I shook my head, thinking, Lord, where do I begin?

I ask myself in all of these cases, what does neighborly love require of me? Jesus said at the end of the parable of the Good Samaritan, "Go and do likewise." Do I have the kind of compassion it takes to let my plans be delayed to stave off the death of a fellow human being—my neighbor? What practical intervention does Christ and His law of love obligate me to provide those left for dead? If I needed help in doing it, what does love demand of you?

CHAPTER THREE

Knowing the Times in Which We Live

To fail to understand what abortion is and to take some measure of its immediate, pervasive, even eternal power to destroy is to misunderstand the times in which we live. America, and most of the world today, is a post-abortion culture. In 1973, the Supreme Court set aside all state abortion restrictions.[1] Since then Americans have intentionally destroyed some sixty million human beings in utero (conservatively estimated). According to the Alan Guttmacher Institute, the research arm associated with Planned Parenthood, the world's largest abortion business, there are forty-two million induced abortions worldwide every year.[2] At current rates, one-third of all American women have at least one abortion by age forty-five.[3] Abortion, then, is the most defining experience of this generation.

The only women among us who have lived through their childbearing years without abortion being both legal and easily accessible across the nation, are eighty-five years old or more. For everyone younger, the right to abortion is all they know. It has become the cornerstone of modernity, in which "choice" and "freedom" mean absolute autonomy from God and His laws. By now, every family in America has been directly affected by abortion (though you may not recognize it).

In its wake, abortion is destroying the health and well-being of women. Dr. David Reardon, one of the nation's leading researchers on the aftereffects of abortion, reports, "Half of all aborted women experience some immediate or long-term physical complications, and almost all suffer from emotional or psychological aftershocks."[4]

Among our family and friends, coworkers, and parishioners, abortion is leading to a host of infections and cancers, while guilt is gnawing away at their souls.[5]

Abortion destroys intimacy. Couples in pregnancy distress, having shared their feelings about why a baby was not in their best interest before the abortion, seldom talk about it afterward. The majority of couples break up subsequent to an abortion. For those that make it, abortion sows seeds of anger, bitterness, shame, and guilt into the marriage. Physical intimacy is stained with bloodguilt. The beauty and mystery of intercourse becomes "ground zero" in a horrific battle against God's procreative grace.

Abortion destroys the essence of femininity. All women are "Eve" (in Hebrew, "mother of all living"), possessing the potential ability to bear life. As one mother who aborted three times told me, "John, never, never forget that a woman is connected to her child by an umbilical cord that is not just physical, but emotional, psychological, and even spiritual. When we murder our own babies, we die as well."

Abortion also destroys masculinity. At the heart of what it means to be a man and not a woman is a sense of leadership in being the provider and protector of women and children. Abortion aborts this sense of responsibility. It weakens a man's self-image as a provider and protector. The spirit of chivalry, which always works in men to the honor of women, is destroyed. It is replaced with the predatory spirit that sees women as "mere equals" to compete with, subdue, and conquer.

Abortion aborts truth and reason as well. We rationalize that abortion could not really be homicide because that would make us, or the people we love who have yielded to abortion, guilty of homicide. We see ourselves as loving and caring people. We would never hurt an innocent child. In fact, we project a self-image that believes we would risk injury to save a child's life. Everyone I know believes he or she is the kind of person who would scream bloody murder if a man took a knife to a baby. Therefore abortion simply cannot involve the murder of a living human being. Our self-image precludes it.

This is why it took hundreds of years and a civil war to face what is now clear to everyone. The people who defended slavery saw themselves as good people who would never hurt or abuse another person. Therefore, their slaves must not be persons, or at least not "full" persons as they are. To admit the truth of abortion, like the truth of slavery, is painful. It will be all the more painful if one hundred years from now, when people look back on the inhumanity of abortion the way we presently look back at the inhumanity of slavery (and in our grief wonder how such moral blindness and civil injustice was allowed to stand in the first place), we find that the church did not take the lead in the abolition movement that is sure to strengthen with each generation to come.

Abortion in the Church

Part of the reason cherishing and defending innocent human life is not a vibrant, conscious, organized mainstream part of the church's mission today is because of our own guilt on the matter. We have aborted our own babies.

Thirty-seven percent of women obtaining abortions identify themselves as Protestant and 28 percent as Catholic.[6] One out of every six abortions are performed on women who identify themselves as "born again" Christians. Indeed, the abortion industry could not survive financially without the paying customers drawn from the church.

In 1989, I was pastoring a small inner-city church in Boston. I was stunned to discover that, by my best estimate, 30 percent of the women in my own congregation had experienced at least one abortion, and some told me of having three and four. I refer to this day of discovery, when as a church family, we looked at the painful truth of abortion for the first time, as "the day God lanced a boil."

Prior to that time, it was common and acceptable for people to confess their involvement with drugs or alcohol or promiscuity or any other sin common in the city of Boston. But nary a word had ever been spoken about abortion. That was the unspeakable sin in our midst. The secrecy, the shame, the fear of discovery all worked to blackmail us into silence and to paralyze the church into inaction. How could we heed the biblical call to cherish and defend innocent human life when we had blood on our own hands?

After the silence was broken, women told me that for years, even as "born again" Christians, they wrestled with self-accusing thoughts like, "What would everyone think of me if they ever learned that I aborted one of my own babies? What would they think of me if they learned that I aborted three of my babies?" Men mirrored similar fear and shame. "What would people think if they knew I paid money to have my own child destroyed?"

Without realizing it, this secret shame was undermining all my preaching efforts to summon forth a bold and muscular Christian faith. This should not have been so surprising to me. The Psalmist testifies that when we cover over our own sin, our strength dries up "as by the heat of summer" (32:4). By the grace of God, we finally uncovered our sin. We faced the painful truth about abortion. And the closest thing to revival that I have ever personally witnessed followed soon after.

As the first-century writer Plutarch said, "Medicine, to produce health, has to examine disease; and music, to create harmony, must investigate discord." A good doctor does not withhold the lance to spare the patient pain. Nor can good physicians of the human soul beg off examining the disease and discord now festering among so many of their own people in their own church. It is spiritual malpractice!

We must lance the boil of this guilt if we are going to produce true health and life. The biggest mistake we are making in our local churches today regarding abortion is rightly sensing its destructive power but then remaining silent to spare people hurt. Gnawing guilt and the whispers of condemnation from the Evil One hurts! Tears of regret heal. Godly sorrow is medicinal.

Make the cut and you will be able to affirm just what the apostle Paul promises will happen when we grieve our sin. "For godly grief produces a repentance that leads to salvation without regret, whereas worldly grief produces death. For see what earnestness this godly grief has produced in you, but also what eagerness to clear yourselves" (2 Cor. 7:10–11).

I witnessed this repentance-born revival in other churches around the world. What God's word says about the shedding of innocent blood is soberly examined. On some occasions, pictures or videos of abortions are shown, revealing why God is so offended by it. Weeping breaks out. There is prayer and confession. Then the cross is preached—the shedding of innocent blood to cover over (atone) for the shedding of innocent blood.

What follows is an earnest desire to get into the fight for life, especially to reach out and rescue the other women and couples. People who have been forgiven much, love much. "Blessed is the one whose transgression is forgiven, whose sin is covered" (Ps. 32:1). When we hide our sin, our strength is drained away. When we uncover it (confess it) and let God cover it instead, through the work of Christ, our strength surges.

This I witnessed up close and personal. Tom served as an elder in my church. When he learned that our leadership had decided to address abortion, he grew unusually cautious and nervous.

As the service drew to a close, I saw his wife, Jane, weeping and Tom sitting absolutely frozen, unable to offer her any comfort. Then, I understood. Through her tears, she haltingly told their secret.

"I have been so angry at Tom all these years for taking me to that abortion clinic," Jane confessed. "It has sown more bitterness in our marriage than anything else." It's not that Jane was shifting all the blame to Tom. She had died a thousand deaths in her own heart over the matter. It's just that a woman always hopes in that situation that her lover will be manly. The hope is that he will protect her rather than expose her to such an unnatural solution. Instead of saying, "Honey, I love you. Our baby will be provided for. I will see to that," Tom escorted her to an abortionist and paid to have the problem go away.

Tom began to weep. "It's my fault. O God, please forgive my sin!" It was a painful time. In the weeks that followed Tom talked openly about his own involvement with abortion and the damage it caused. At one point, his testimony changed. He had taken his wife for two abortions before they were married. Later still, his testimony changed again. He had aborted three of his children.

So deep and painful was the truth that God in His grace had to peel away the shame in layers over time rather than all at once. If you want to understand the times in which we live, and how abortion guilt is quenching the spirit of grace and power in our people, just ask those who have aborted to quietly seek you out.

There is no therapy, no steps program, no psychological cure for the guilt of abortion. Only the innocent blood of Christ, proclaimed and believed, can cleanse away the bloodguilt of abortion. So the matter comes full circle. We live in a time when people have blood-stained consciences and need a blood-shedding solution, which is the cross itself.[7] Those who preach the gospel without ever mentioning abortion by name (pastors like me!) unwittingly lead the very people they love and serve to interpret their silence to mean that abortion is the unforgivable sin.

That is why I, too, needed to repent. I was collaborating with death by my silence. My repentance led to an earnestness in me as well. We led a Boston-wide, multi-church, Christian effort to help women in pregnancy distress. We organized a small army of worker bees to come alongside new mothers and bird-dog young fathers. Some they helped get married. Others they helped find employment or figure out how to stay in school. They had to meet with disappointed parents. They had to start helping each mother develop a parenting plan. We came to call this work, "cross-bearing for the childbearing." Babies were saved and many young mothers and couples learned to pray and trust in God through it all.

Abortion as a Youth-Oriented Business

To understand the times in which we live we must also understand that abortion is not just something people resort to because of personally embarrassing or difficult circumstances. Abortion is also a business with a full marketing plan. Twenty percent of abortions are performed on teenagers. They are targeted for abortion. In her pamphlet *Selling Teen Abortions*, Carol Everett, who once ran lucrative abortion facilities in Texas (before becoming a Christian changed her life), recounts the deceptive way she marketed abortion to teenagers. Using the public school system and the false promise of contraception, she promoted sexual activity. This, after all, is the only way to get more pregnancies and therefore sell more abortions. Asked how she did this, she writes:

> I established myself with the teens as an authority on sex. I explained to them that their parents wouldn't help them with their sexuality, but I would. I separated them from their support system, number one, and they listened to me. Second, our doctors prescribed low dose birth control pills with a high pregnancy rate, knowing well that they needed to be taken very accurately at the same time every day or pregnancy would occur.

> This insured the teens to be my best customers as teenagers typically are not responsible enough to follow such rigid medication guidelines on their own. I

knew their sexual activity would increase from none or once a week to five or seven times a week once they were introduced to this contraception method. Then I could reach my goal—three to five abortions for each teenager between the ages of 13 and 18.[8]

Obviously, unrepentant abortionists would deny such base motives. Advocates of legal abortion constantly seek to switch the debate away from abortion to contraception and voice their desire to avoid pregnancies. Some, no doubt, naively believe their own "let's-promote-contraception-to-make-abortion-rare" mantra. But the evidence shows that contraception does not make abortion rare.

According to the Alan Guttmacher Institute (AGI), an organization strongly affiliated with Planned Parenthood, 54 percent of all women seeking an abortion report that they were using birth control during the month that they became pregnant.[9]

Moreover, abortion itself is a form of birth control. According to both the Centers for Disease Control (CDC) and AGI, 45 percent of all abortions are repeat abortions.[10] According the data collected by the National Abortion Federation, one in four women (26 percent to be exact) seeking an abortion have had an earlier abortion.[11] As if to belie claims that abortions are somehow "necessary" for these women, both government and abortion industry data show that more than 93 percent of all induced abortions are done on perfectly healthy mothers with perfectly healthy babies.[12]

Abortion is big business. At the same time that they profess a desire to make abortion "rare," Planned Parenthood pushes abortion "sales." Former Planned Parenthood clinic director Abby Johnson says that she was given an "abortion quota" and was instructed by her superiors to double the number of abortion sales in order to bring in more revenue.[13] Planned Parenthood now brings in over $1 billion a year in income. According to their most recent report, for fiscal years 2009–2010, abortion patients constitute 12 percent of their clients—that is 332,000 of 3 million unduplicated clients. Thirty-seven percent of their income revenue is from abortion procedures, according to conservative estimates. Planned Parenthood has issued a directive instructing that all affiliates must have at least one clinic that performs abortion by 2013.[14] The abortion industry hardly seems intent on making abortion rare.

The more its supporters promote contraception rather than abstinence before and virtue within marriage, the more abortions and "unplanned pregnancies" we experience. Christ told us that we would know a tree by the fruit it bears. Widespread acceptance of contraception has fueled rampant non-marital sexual activity, radically higher divorce rates, the use of women as sex objects, and millions of abortion deaths.

Abortion among Minorities

One pastoral associate of mine in Boston, a well-respected black minister, upon learning about the pregnancy help centers opening in Boston, said, "Well, abortion is not a problem in our church. Our people don't have abortions." This is woeful ignorance and wishful thinking. According to one study, "Abortion Attitudes in the African American Community," this is a strongly believed myth in the black community. According to the study:

> Abortion is viewed by many African Americans as a "white problem"—particularly among men. There appears to be a strong perception that white women are far more likely to have abortions than are African American women. We frequently heard men say, "Our women do not have abortions." While recognizing that abortions occur somewhat more frequently [than the rate expected by men], women also seemed to believe that it was a choice of last resort.[15]

When informed about the actual abortion statistics, many African Americans are appalled. Black women make up only 12 percent of women of childbearing age, but they account for 30 percent of all abortions. Hispanic women constitute only 13 percent of this same group, but suffer 20 percent of the total abortions in America. Together, these two minority groups account for 25 percent of women of childbearing age in America but account for

55 percent of the total babies aborted in the country.[16] In other words, minority women are aborting at more than twice the rate of white women, and the leading cause of death in the black community is abortion.

And in specific cities the data is shocking. Fifty-seven percent of black pregnancies in New York City end in abortion, according to 2009 data from the city's Department of Health.[17] For white women, the number is 20 percent and for the city overall it is about 39 percent.

A growing number of black Christian leaders are openly calling this black genocide.[18] African-American pastor Bishop Joseph L. Garlington has led Covenant Church in Pittsburgh since 1971, and is a true pastor to pastors. I asked him if he thought genocide was an overstatement. He replied:

> No, I do not. I don't think that's an overstatement at all. To me this issue is spiritual warfare. My grandson Jacob [adopted at birth] has just finished his first year in college. He's got tremendous artistic skills and I can think where would Jacob be if his mom and dad hadn't cared for him? So Jacob becomes part of an army of creative people that God can use because they are alive. And I think the whole issue of genocide, particularly among African-Americans, is a very real issue.[19]

His church recently established the Women's Choice Network pregnancy help center in his predominantly black neighborhood (Wilkinsburg).

Adding to this tragedy, in public surveys of abortion, minority women poll as more "pro-life" than white women. I tremble to think of what that means in terms of suffering the guilt and trauma of abortion. These are the times in which we live. Now let us turn and consider what God would have us do.

CHAPTER FOUR

God's Passion for Life

*I*n all things, God is preeminent. We love because He loved us first. He calls us to be holy because He is holy. He loves justice and wants us eager to see justice done. In the same way, our passionate commitment to cherish and defend innocent human life directly flows from God's own passionate commitment.

God is life. "Whoever finds *me* finds *life*" (Prov. 8:35). God upholds life (Ps. 54:4), preserves life (Gen. 45:5), and restores life (Ruth 4:15). He is the light of life (Job 33:30), the keeper of life (Ps. 121:7), the fountain of life (Prov. 14:27), and the redeemer of life (Ps. 72:14).

Pursuing Him is the path of life (Ps. 16:11). Fearing Him prolongs life (Prov. 10:27). Unity with others before God is so sweet that it is called "life forevermore" (Ps. 133:3). It is good to cry with the Psalmist, "Give me life according to your word!"(119:25).[1]

Simply put, "life is God's gift to the world."[2] In sending Jesus Christ into the world, God brings us the message of life (Acts 5:20), the light of life (John 8:12), abundant Life (John 10:10), and the words of everlasting life (John 6:68).

To love God is to love life. To be Christlike is to be for life. The historian George Grant writes, "The pro-life movement and the Christian faith are synonymous. Where there is one, there will be the other—for one cannot be had without the other."[3]

God's creation is swarming with life. Man's first assignment in the garden was "to work it and keep it" (Gen. 2:15). He did this in part by naming the things around him. In naming things, Adam grew in understanding of the wonder of life around him (2:19–20). All the natural sciences begin here, categorizing things into their differing phyla and species and families.

In naming livestock, the birds of the air, the beasts of the field, and the fish in the seas, he came to understand himself as well. He was superior over the rest of creation, and he was in solitude. There was nothing like him, suited for him, in God's creation (2:20). So God continued to create life, only this time to create someone uniquely suited to Adam and from which human life would multiply and fill the earth to the joy and glory of God.

Among all forms of life, God especially treasures human life. On one occasion, the Pharisees tried to entangle Jesus in controversy over paying taxes. They asked Him, "Is it lawful to pay taxes to Caesar or not?" Jesus told the Pharisees to look on the coin used for taxes and tell Him whose image was on it. "Caesar's," they replied. Then Jesus said, "Render to Caesar the things that are Caesar's, and to God the things that are God's" (Matt. 22:21). In saying this, Jesus pointed to what God endows with a possessive love and claims for Himself as Sovereign Ruler. What is it that has God's image stamped onto it and, by this imprint, should be rendered unto God alone? The answer, of course, is human life.

We assert that all human life is sacred and belongs to God because all people are made in the image of God (Gen. 1:27). Since every human being is created by God and in His image, every human being has intrinsic rather than relative value. People are not valued according to their quality of life or their usefulness to serve the desires of others. They are not to be destroyed when "unwanted" by us. God, in making them, wants them. They are not to be discarded, sacrificed, or euthanized because they are useless to others. They have sovereign use to God.

The moral offense of abortion begins here. Like all other forms of homicide, it is an act that defaces the glory of God reflected in the life God is shaping for His own glory. Abortion destroys God's property, something He made for His own good purposes.

Among all human life, God especially cherishes innocent human life. He calls repeatedly for us to respect and defend the innocent.[4] "Do not kill the innocent and righteous, for I will not acquit the wicked" (Exod. 23:7). "Acquitting the innocent and condemning the guilty" is the standard of justice God requires of judges who preside in our courts (Deut. 25:1). "It is not good to be partial to the wicked or to deprive the righteous of justice" (Prov. 18:5). "Woe to those who . . . acquit the guilty for a bribe, and deprive the innocent of his right!" (Isa. 5:22–23).

Among all forms of innocent human life, God especially treasures children. This quality is one that we, under normal circumstances, understand quite well. In Boston, when I lived there, a three-year-old boy was shot to death while his father was fending off a home invader. The city was shaken. It made a difference that it was a child who was killed. "He was an innocent *child!*" people lamented. Of course it is wicked to shed any innocent blood. God takes it personally and will have His day of vengeance. He will indict them saying, "You have fattened your hearts in a day of slaughter. You have condemned and murdered the righteous person" (James 5:5–6). But we sense an increased moral offense at the killing an innocent child, because children by definition have not hurt or offended anyone in any way. They represent innocence in our fallen world.

Christ acknowledges this sense of innocence regarding children. One of His sharpest warnings came when He considered how people injure and rob children of their innocence when they introduce them to sin. "Whoever causes one of these little ones who believe in me to sin, it would be better for him to have a great millstone fastened around his neck and to be drowned in the depth of the sea" (Matt. 18:6). Clearly the innocence of children is precious in His sight.

Among all the ways that innocent children bring delight, God especially delights in fashioning children in the womb. Psalm 139:13–14 says, "You formed my inward parts; you knitted me together in my mother's womb. I praise you, for I am fearfully and wonderfully made." In this verse, David considers his own pre-born life. He sees a "me" in there being made personally by a divine "you." David views his mother's womb as God's personal art studio and praises Him for it. Gestation is God designing each one of us into a one-of-a-kind human being.

When you look elsewhere in the Bible, you see the same thing. Our lives as human beings begin in the womb. One example is found in Genesis 4:1: "Now Adam knew Eve his wife, and she conceived and bore Cain." In the view of Scripture, it was the *person*, Cain, who was conceived and the *person*, Cain, who was born. Dr. John Davis, professor of theology at Gordon-Conwell Theological Seminary, observes, "The writer's interest in Cain extends back beyond his birth, to his conception. That is when his personal history begins."[5] From the moment of conception the humanity and personhood—the life—of Cain began.

The same is true of Job's life. He also saw his personal history as beginning at conception. He said, "Let the day perish on which I was born, and the night that said, 'A man is conceived'" (Job 3:3). What was conceived? Not a potential human being, not something abstract or short of personhood, but a male human being was conceived.

In the worldview of the Bible, children are children whether inside a womb or inside a house. Genesis 25:22 says of Rebekah, "The *children* struggled together within her." Throughout the Old Testament, the Hebrew word for children is the same, whether referring to children inside or outside the womb. In the New Testament, the word used to refer to an unborn baby (the Greek word *brephos*), is the same word used for a newborn baby. In Luke 1:44, Elizabeth refers to the "baby in my womb." This is the same word used in Luke 2:12 for the newborn baby Jesus, "You will find a baby wrapped in swaddling cloths and lying in a manger."

Retired pastor and campus minister Clifford Bajema summarizes the biblical view of human life. He writes, "Scripture does not make the kind of subtle philosophical distinctions people make so often today between human life and human being, man and person, life and Life. Scripture just talks about man."[6]

Consider also the conception and birth of Jesus Christ. The angel Gabriel announces to the young virgin Mary that she will conceive a son and give birth to a son, by the Holy Spirit (Luke 1:31). Mary submits in wonder to this astonishing news and offers herself to God and His service (1:38). Then she immediately heads off to visit her relative Elizabeth who, as Mary also learned from Gabriel, was six months pregnant. Elizabeth's child we will come to know as John the Baptist. Thirty years later as an adult he will announce the coming of the promised Messiah with strong and prophetic words: "Prepare the way of the Lord" (3:4). But this is not the first time he actually welcomed the arrival of the Son of God.

When Mary arrives at Elizabeth's home, Elizabeth perceives that Mary is now pregnant and shouts her praises, "Blessed is the fruit of your womb!" (Luke 1:42). Then a little bit of womb to womb worship breaks out. "When Elizabeth heard the greeting of Mary, the baby leaped in her womb. . . . [Elizabeth said] when the sound of your greeting came to my ears, the baby in my womb leaped for joy" (1:41, 44). The unborn baby, John the Baptist, probably under the influence of the Holy Spirit that filled Elizabeth at that very moment (1:41), rejoiced in being in the presence of the unborn child, Jesus Christ the Almighty!

Now consider how far along Christ was at this moment in terms of His embryonic development. Follow the time line. Mary is told that she will conceive a son. Luke 1:39 says that she immediately "arose and went with *haste* into the hill country, to a town in Judah, and she entered the house of Zechariah and greeted Elizabeth." When she arrived at the house, she had conceived a son. She was pregnant.[7] The travel time is perhaps a day or two, but let's say, even traveling with haste, that it took a week. When the unborn baby John welcomed the incarnate son of God, who is human, in all ways like us (but without sin), Christ is developmentally, a mere zygote, perhaps smaller than the period at the end of this sentence.

If that strikes you as unusual, it is not. It is perfectly normal. You and everyone you know were once that small. The way you looked at three months or at birth or when you became a teenager or as you look today is just a continuation of natural human development that began at fertilization. All that is different is time and nourishment.

CHAPTER FIVE

Healing for the Morally Blind

I n truth, we all know what a human being is. I have never heard a mother give birth and wonder, "Is my baby a real human being yet?" Human life is self-evident. Legal abortion, like legal slavery in the past, requires us to suppress what is self-evident. We can see plainly what biology merely defines in more detail, unless self-interest gets in the way. When it does, then sophistry kicks in and we invent ways to see evil as good. In 1787 we proposed the notion that some human beings were only three-fifths of a person and that slavery was not only good, but good for them. Today we are doing the same thing with the unborn.

So what is the unborn? The science of embryology is well established. "Human embryos are not creatures different in kind from human beings," writes Robert P. George of Princeton University. "They are, rather, like human beings—distinct living members of the species Homo sapiens—at the earliest stage of their natural development. They differ from human beings at later developmental stages not in virtue of the kind of entity they are, but rather by degree of development."[1] You did not start as an embryo and then grow into a human being. You matured as a human being through the embryonic stage to your current one.

Your life, as a distinct, living, and whole human being, began at conception.[2] Every single biology textbook in the world agrees with this. For example, Keith Moore and T. V. N. Persaud, in *The Developing Human: Clinically Oriented Embryology*, write, "Human development begins at fertilization when a male gamete or sperm (spermatozoon) unites with a female gamete or oocyte (ovum) to form a single cell—a zygote. This highly specialized, totipotent cell marked the beginning of each of us as a unique individual."[3] From there we develop in a distinct and clear pattern through various stages of maturation (zygote, embryo, fetus, newborn, child, adolescent, adult, senior, etc.).

The wonderful science of embryology, together with advances in technology, especially ultrasound, have allowed us to see, photograph, and film in living color what King David so poetically meditated upon in Psalm 139:13–14. "You knit me together in my mother's womb. I praise you because I am fearfully and wonderfully made" (NIV).

At fertilization, all human chromosomes are present and a unique human life begins. After six days the embryo begins implanting in the uterus. The baby's heart starts beating as early as the eighteenth day, with the child's own blood, which is often a different blood type than the mother's. This is about the same time that a woman misses her period and wonders if she is pregnant. Surgical abortions are usually not performed before seven weeks (49 days from the first day of a woman's last menstrual period). By that time, the baby has identifiable arms and legs (day 45) and has measurable brain waves (about 40 days). During the seventh through the tenth weeks, when 62 percent of all abortions are performed, fingers and genitals appear and the child's face is recognizably human. At six weeks all the major organs are formed, and by twelve weeks no new anatomical developments occur. The baby is only growing bigger.[4]

Yet in this country there are 280 abortions performed *every day* on babies that are thirteen weeks gestation or more.[5] They are not done to save the life of the mother. They are done for the same reasons earlier abortions are done. The right to abortion, as it stands now, allows a woman to abort her baby at any time for any reason or no reason.[6]

Dr. Bernard Nathanson (1926–2011) was responsible for seventy-five thousand abortions in New York in the late 1960s and early 1970s. He was one of the main architects of strategies designed to legalize abortion in America. It was ultrasound, invented in the 1970s, that became for him a window to the womb. He wrote:

> From then on we could see this person in the womb from the very beginning—and study and measure it and weigh it and take care of it and treat it and diagnose it and do all kinds of things. It became, in essence, a second patient. Now a patient is a person. So basically I was dealing then with two people, instead of just one carrying some lump of meat around. That's what started me doubting the ethical acceptability of abortion on request.[7]

Dr. Nathanson's acknowledgement of the humanity of the unborn child had no conscious religious tone to it. Dr. Nathanson was an atheistic Jew. "I had not a seedling of faith to nourish me," he wrote.[8] Embryology itself, confirmed by ultrasound, led him to acknowledge the humanity of unborn children.

The New England Journal of Medicine reported back in 1983 that ultrasound was teaching doctors to see the unborn child as a "patient."

> Ultrasound imagery will probably change the way in which we view the fetus with a diagnosed and treatable disorder . . . Indeed, surgeons already regard the fetus with a correctable congenital defect as a "patient."[9]

The same report also indicated that ultrasound examinations were turning ambivalent mothers toward parenthood and away from abortion.

One of us pointed to the small, visibly moving fetal form on the screen and asked, "How do you feel about seeing what is inside you?" She answered crisply, "It certainly makes you think twice about abortion! . . . I feel that it is human. It belongs to me. I could never have an abortion now."

Defenders of legal abortion who acknowledge the embryological science of human life then shift to philosophical grounds. They make a distinction between what it means to be a human and what it means to be a person with rights and protections.[10]

My friend and co-author Scott Klusendorf, president of Life Training Institute, has helped many of us to think through the philosophical justifications posited by abortion advocates and, in response, to articulate a philosophical and rational defense that shows that there is no morally significant difference between the embryo that you once were and the adult that you are today that would justify killing you at that early stage of development.

There are mainly four arguments used to suggest otherwise: differences of size, level of development, environment, and degree of dependency. Using the simple acronym SLED, Klusendorf presents the philosophical defense of unborn human life. Here is a brief summary:

Size: True, embryos are smaller than newborns and adults, but why is that relevant? Do we really want to say that large people are more human than small ones? Men are generally larger than women, but that doesn't mean that they deserve more rights. Size doesn't equal value.

Level of development: True, embryos and fetuses are less developed than the adults they'll one day become. But again, why is this relevant? Four-year-old girls are less developed than fourteen-year-old ones. Should older children have more rights than their younger siblings? Some people say that self-awareness makes one human. But if that is true, newborns do not qualify as valuable human beings. Six-week-old infants lack the immediate capacity for performing human mental functions, as do the reversibly comatose, the sleeping, and those with Alzheimer's Disease.

Environment: Where you are has no bearing on who you are. Does your value change when you cross the street or roll over in bed? If not, how can a journey of eight inches down the birth-canal suddenly change the essential nature of the unborn from nonhuman to human? If the unborn are not already human, merely changing their location can't make them valuable.

Degree of Dependency: If viability makes us human, then all those who depend on insulin or kidney medication are not valuable and we may kill them. Conjoined twins who share blood type and bodily systems also have no right to life.

In short, it's far more reasonable to argue that although humans differ immensely with respect to talents, accomplishments, and degrees of development, they are nonetheless equal because they share a common human nature.[11]

The Eclipse of Reason

Corrupt language, and you corrupt thought. Corrupt the meaning of "personhood," and you can rationalize abortion. Bernard Nathanson noted that the applied language of personhood has always been exclusive in history. During the Holocaust, Jews (as well as Gypsies and Poles and Roman Catholic priests) were widely classified as nonpersons. Likewise, blacks in America suffered the same treatment under the infamous Dred Scott ruling that upheld the practice of slavery.

So today, justifying elective abortion requires redefinition and schizophrenic reasoning or, as Nathanson calls it, "The eclipse of reason."

If a drunk driver kills a mother on her way to the hospital for a prenatal checkup, the killer can be charged with a double homicide. Yet if she makes it safely to the hospital but changes her mind about having another child, she can have the baby removed piece by piece or delivered breech in the ghastly infanticide procedure misnamed the "partial birth" abortion.

In Massachusetts, a pregnant mother was put in jail because the Department of Social Services feared she might hurt her unborn baby. She belonged to a small religious sect that did not believe in using modern medicine and hospitals in caring for their children. The State argued that they had a compelling interest to protect the health of the unborn baby and make sure the baby got medical help upon delivery if need be. Yet if this mother declared her "reproductive rights" and insisted on an abortion, they would have taken her to an abortion facility. In Massachusetts, the State would even have had to pay for it.

In the summer of 2000, a flurry of e-mail arrived telling me about an astounding picture of a human hand. In the photo, a twenty-one-week-old unborn, Samuel Alexander Armes, reaches out from his mother's womb to clasp the finger of the surgeon who is about to save his life. Baby Samuel, undergoing surgery for spina bifida, had yet to take his first breath—yet his grip, so sure and firm, spoke loudly. "I am here. I am alive. I am counting on you. I am grateful."

For a moment, the nation understood what Sir Charles Bell, one of the most respected comparative anatomists of the nineteenth century, once declared: "No serious account of human life can ignore the importance of the human hand."

"The human hand is so beautifully formed," observed Bell, "its actions are so powerful, so free and yet so delicate, that there is no thought of its complexity as an instrument; we use it as we draw our breath, unconsciously."[12]

Bell was providing an early rebuttal to Darwin's theory of evolution at the time. Divine proportion was at work. In the human hand, the Perfect Craftsman wrote His signature.

Little baby Samuel's hand gripping the surgeon's glove woke the conscience of a nation, be it ever so briefly, that the unborn is self-evidently a human being. Look at the picture! Abortion is self-evidently the violent destruction of a human being. This truth I have carried with me for some years, strangely, in the form of a human hand. In 1989, a friend of mine pulled a tiny hand from the rubbish behind my local abortion facility. If the first picture is a wonder, the second is a crime against humanity. If baby Samuel's little grip says, "Thank you!" what does this unnamed baby's hand say but, "I am here, too. Won't someone save my life? Why are they hurting me?"

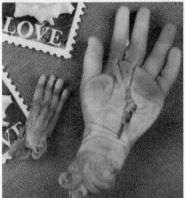

Photo: Michael Clancy. Used by permission.

CHAPTER SIX

The Injustice of Abortion and the Just Anger of God

*A*bortion represents the preeminent evil of our time. In saying this I am challenging the widespread notion that it is just one issue among equals—homelessness, fatherlessness, hunger—that the Christian community ought to deal with on an equal footing.

No, it is not. Christians can and should actively engage in alleviating the suffering that comes from chronic poverty and disease. The hungry must be fed. Orphans must be cared for. The sick and the dying need tending to. The church knows this and has a glorious history of doing all this and more.[1] Most of the relief work in the world today has Christian roots and every year new nonprofit ministries are started to address particular needs in particular places.

But abortion is not in the same category any more than a man storming a high school with a machine gun is equal to a teenager in the school not having enough lunch money. One represents the chronic problem of poverty. The other represents a violent act of evil.

I do not say that abortion is the only injustice deserving our attention. I say it is a preeminent injustice that calls for an urgent response.[2] Part of the problem in saying this persuasively is that the word *abortion* simply cannot convey its true injustice or moral offense. In fact, the descriptive is so benign that it has the effect of reducing and masking both.[3]

The late Dr. Bernard Nathanson, who helped legalize abortion in America and lived to regret and renounce it, tried his best to convey what we are up against. He wrote:

> The abortion holocaust is beyond the ordinary discourse of morality and rational condemnation. It is not enough to pronounce it absolutely evil . . . The abortion tragedy is a new event, severed from connections with traditional presuppositions of history, psychology, politics, and morality. It extends beyond the deliberations of reason, beyond the discernment of moral judgment, beyond meaning itself . . . This is an evil torn free of its moorings in reason and causality, an ordinary secular corruption raised to unimaginable powers of magnification and limitless extremity.[4]

Abortion shares the same mind-numbing, too-horrifying-to-be-true quality that the specter of the Holocaust raised for previous generations. The numbers are now so large and the implications of our guilt so great that we experience something of an intellectual coma from the trauma of it. We simply shut down.

Abortion justly invokes the anger of a loving God toward those who participate in it or those who make peace with it. Let me explain why.

Among all the offenses of man, the greatest offense is shedding innocent blood. God is long-suffering. But there is a limit to His patience. There is a point when, through the hardness of our hearts, we become so callous to the moral beauty and righteousness of God that He says, "Enough!" In Noah's time, the level of evil reached that point. "Then the LORD said, 'My Spirit shall not contend with man forever'" (Gen. 6:3 alternate reading). Then He wiped the earth clean in righteous judgment (6:7).

In tracing out the breaking point when God moves from patiently warning to active judgment, Scripture says it is the "abomination" of shedding innocent blood, either by killing innocent people or passively accepting the killing of innocent people, that finally invokes His wrath.

This is the message of the prophets. Some prophets brought this message as an indictment for the judgment about to befall them. Others brought

it as a reminder to the people as to why they experienced God's judgment. In both cases, they pointed
to the shedding of innocent blood as the point
when God's patience reached its end and He said,
"Enough!" Consider the prophet Ezekiel:

> Thus says the Lord GOD: A city that sheds blood
> in her midst, so that her time may come, and that
> makes idols to defile herself! You have become guilty
> by the blood that you have shed, and defiled by the
> idols that you have made, and you have brought your
> days near, the appointed time of your years has come.
> Therefore I have made you a reproach to the nations,
> and a mockery to all the countries (Ezek. 22:3–4).

The prophet Isaiah also declared that the time
had arrived when Israel's rejection of the righteousness of God reached a breaking point. What they
were doing was so wretched in God's eyes that He
declared, "Enough! Don't even bother to call on My
name anymore. I am done listening." Isaiah records
it this way, "When you spread out your hands, I
will hide my eyes from you; even though you make
many prayers, I will not listen." What was it that
Israel was doing that so offended God that He broke
off His desire to hear their prayers? Isaiah answers,
"Your hands are full of blood. Wash yourselves;
make yourselves clean" (Isa. 1:15–16).

God protects what He loves (just as you do).
What He loves in creation is His people, as I sus-
pect is true in your case. When His moral precepts

that protect human life are violated, God is rightly angered. In Genesis 4:10, we catch a glimpse of how earnestly God cares for innocent human life and how angry He becomes when we destroy it. Cain killed his brother Abel. God confronts Cain saying, "Listen! Your brother's blood cries out to me from the ground."

In Revelation, we read of those who were murdered because of their faith in Christ. God's judgment is described as just retribution. "You are just in these judgments . . . for they have shed the blood of your saints and prophets" (16:5–6 NIV).

Because God loves, He gets angry. Because He cherishes innocent human life with a burning heart, He commands all men everywhere to do the same. His revulsion at the murder of the innocents knows no limit, nor does His wrath when it is finally unleashed. God's wrath is called "fierce" (1 Sam. 28:18), furious (Job 40:11), "full" (Ps. 78:38 NIV), consuming (Ps. 59:13), "great" (Ps. 102:10 NIV), and "jealous" (Ezek. 36:6). For God to warn us of His wrath is another sign of His love. For us to ignore it is another sign of how hardened we have become—how ripe we are to receive His wrath and how just God is in rendering it.

Among all the ways men shed innocent blood, the most offensive is child sacrifice. There are many ways to shed innocent blood, but the most heinous form, the most morally offensive, is child sacrifice. In child sacrifice, what God cherishes and protects is intentionally destroyed, *and at the same time* God's glory, the radiance of His own moral perfection, is directly impugned. Instead of being proclaimed through the earth as the God who cherishes and defends human life, He is reduced to a false god who demands the murder of innocent babies out of some pernicious bloodlust.

One cannot profane the glory of God by any greater means. So Israel was instructed, "Do not give any of your children to be sacrificed to Molech, for you must not *profane* the name of your God. I am the Lord" (Lev 18:21 niv).

In God's eyes, both child sacrifice and the passive acceptance of child sacrifice profane God's name and arouse His indignation. So He taught the people of Israel:

> Say to the people of Israel, Any one of the people of Israel or of the strangers who sojourn in Israel who gives any of his children to Molech shall surely be put to death . . . I myself will set my face against that man and will cut him off from among his people, because he has given one of his children to Molech, to make my sanctuary unclean and to profane my holy name. And if the people of the land do at all close their eyes to that man when he gives one of his children to Molech, and do not put him to death, then I will set my face against that man and against his clan and will cut them off from among their people, him and all who follow him in whoring after Molech. (Lev. 20:2–5)

Israel was to have no part in the shedding of innocent blood of children. They were to avoid it and oppose it as the very antithesis of what pleases the true and living God.

God also warned Israel that if they followed the same practices of the people He was wiping off the land, they too would be wiped away (for God treats all men equally before His holy law). When God wanted to emphasize what sort of practices were to be avoided, and what it was particularly that so offended Him and finally invoked His unrestrained wrath, what did He point to? He pointed again to the shedding of innocent blood of children.

Deuteronomy 12:31 says, "You shall not worship the LORD your God in that way, for every abominable thing that the LORD hates they have done for their gods, for they even burn their sons and their daughters in the fire to their gods."

Notice the word *even*. This is God's way of pointing out how extreme the evil was that now justly ended His patience. The hardness of their hearts against the will and pleasure of the living and true God was so hard and perverted that they *even* cut the throat of innocent babies thinking that this would please the perverse desires of the god of their own making. Child sacrifice unites murder with idolatry. It destroys the image of God in a way that defames the goodness of God.

In spite of these warnings, Israel did come to a point in their history where they become so insensitive to God that they even imitated this abomination. Ahaz, king of Judah, "did not do what was right in the eyes of the LORD his God, as his father David had done, but he walked in the way of the kings of Israel. He *even* burned his son as an offering, according to the despicable practices of the nations whom the LORD drove out before the people of Israel" (2 Kings 16:2–3).

Ahaz comes to represent the pinnacle of moral corruption in Israel. Why? Because he reached the pinnacle of moral offense: He *even* slaughtered his own innocent child and offered his son up to demons, in the name of God.

Why do I say Ahaz offered his son to demons, though he convinced himself that it was a divine sacrifice? Because this is the power that lies behind child sacrifice. Psalm 106:37–38 says, "They sacrificed their sons and their daughters *to the demons*; they poured out innocent blood, the blood of their sons and daughters, whom they sacrificed to the idols of Canaan, and the land was polluted with blood."

Israel and Judah both suffered the judgment of God for their idolatrous sacrifice of innocent children. The kingdom of Israel was wiped out first. "The king of Assyria invaded all the land . . . [and] captured Samaria, and he carried the Israelites away to Assyria" (2 Kings 17:5–6). The people were not left to wonder why. This took place "because the people of Israel had sinned against the LORD their God" (17:7). What sins had they committed? A list follows. Last on the list, the final expression of divine disgust, is this: "They burned their sons and their daughters as offerings and used divination and omens and sold themselves to do evil in the sight of the LORD, provoking him to anger" (17:17).

Perhaps the clearest expression of God's outrage against the slaughter of innocent children is found in Ezekiel 16:20–21. Here child sacrifice is recorded in very personal terms. "And you took your sons and your daughters, whom you had borne to *me*, and these you sacrificed to them to be devoured. Were your whorings so small a matter that you slaughtered *my* children and delivered them up as an offering by fire to them?"

God takes the slaughter of innocent children as nothing less than the murder of His own children.

Abortion is child sacrifice. Whatever the reasons we cling to in order to justify abortion, they are no match for what the conscience knows and Scripture confirms is "child sacrifice." We want our lives to go according to our plans. The baby is sacrificed to secure them. Kim Flodin, a staunch defender of abortion rights and a freelance writer, had two abortions. She wrote of her anguishing circumstances and subsequent guilt and injuries for *Newsweek* magazine. She concluded, "I was pregnant, I carried two unborn children and I chose, for completely selfish reasons, to deny them life so that I could better my own."[5] This is child sacrifice.

We no longer sacrifice our children to please some pagan, bloodthirsty god like Molech. We have made ourselves into a god and sacrifice our children for our own ends. We abort because of money, believing we cannot afford a child and do the other things we want to do with our money. We abort to save ourselves the embarrassment of others discovering our promiscuity and to save our reputations. We abort to save relationships or educational and vocational goals we have planned. There are many understandable reasons for abortion. But they are all penultimate reasons. The ultimate reason we abort is selfishness and a lack of faith in God. Or as James 4:2 says, "You want something but don't get it. You kill and covet, but you cannot have what you want" (NIV). Not everyone comes to see it as honestly as Kim Flodin does, but that in a nutshell is what abortion is all about. Abortion is killing so that we may get something else. As such, abortion is a substitute for prayer. [6] "You do not have, because you do not ask God."

But there is one difference between child sacrifice as performed in biblical times and abortion today. Child sacrifice was more humane. One swift cut and the deed was done. Abortion is multiple lacerations and limbs pulled off piece by piece, in a blind surgical process, while the baby is still alive. It is so graphic that video and pictures of abortion are as difficult to see as anything coming out of Dachau in the 1940s, or beheadings in the Middle East today.[7]

CHAPTER SEVEN

Commitments That Answer the Call

How, then, shall we live? What must we do if we are to hold each life precious? What does God call us to do? What does answering the call look like?

I think answering the call involves a four-fold commitment.

1. Commit to not shedding innocent blood yourself. This law has been written on every human heart, in every culture, in every age. Every branch of Christianity agrees that "the sacredness of life gives rise to its inviolability, written from the beginning in man's heart . . . in the depths of his conscience, man is always reminded of the inviolability of life—his own life and that of others—as something which does not belong to him, because it is the property and gift of God the Creator and Father."[1]

In opposing abortion, we are not imposing a morality distinctive to Christianity. We are defending the common justice due to all people of every race and of every faith (or no faith). Every human being innately desires his life to be respected. The right to life is the foundation for both civil justice and peace, making way for the freedom to choose what we perceive promises us the most happiness. But it is in that order, life, then liberty, in the pursuit of happiness.

What rings true as natural law is amplified in the Ten Commandments. Exodus 20:13 says simply, "You shall not murder." God protects what He loves, just as you do. Human life, being God's chief delight in His creation, is protected by His moral law.

Virginia Ramey Mollenkott, professor emerita at William Paterson University in New Jersey, claims that "nowhere does the Bible prohibit abortion."[2] In one sense she is right. The word *abortion* does not appear in the Bible. Of course, she is asserting, without defending, a notion that whatever the Bible explicitly fails to condemn, it must condone. Nowhere does the Bible prohibit "lynching" or "domestic violence" or "infanticide." In recent years, the word "gendercide" has been introduced. It refers to the killing of baby girls in countries like China and India. By her own logic, Mollenkott would have to approve of these atrocities. She would not of course.[3]

The Bible teaches that abortion is unjust by teaching us that the unborn child is a human being and calling us to protect all human life from homicide. What is more, the Bible teaches us to work extra hard at protecting the unborn child by calling us to work extra hard at protecting the *rights* of defenseless human beings. "*Give justice* to the weak and the fatherless; *maintain the right* of the afflicted and the destitute" (Ps. 82:3).

Are there any exceptions to this rule? What about people conceived by rape or incest? Isn't abortion an appropriate remedy in such painful cases? But let's rephrase the question: How should we treat innocent human beings that remind us of a painful event? That one question gets to the heart of the matter.[4]

You have to be cruel beyond measure not to ache for victims of sexual violence and want to relieve their suffering. But compassion means to "suffer with" others. So we need to be careful that we are not coming up with a solution that makes us feel better, but not them. Encouraging a woman to kill her innocent unborn baby is not doing something helpful or healthy *for her*. More often than not, it increases her suffering. As one woman reported:

> I soon discovered that the aftermath of my abortion continued a long time after the memory of my rape had faded. I felt empty and horrible. Nobody told me about the pain I would feel deep within causing nightmares and deep depressions. They had all told me that after the abortion I could continue my life as if nothing had happened.[5]

Victims of sexual assault more often than not sense this reality.[6] Close to three out of four victims of sexual assault resulting in pregnancy *do not have abortions*. They have their babies.[7]

Why? At its base is the truth that the external circumstance under which a child is conceived does not cancel that child's inherent worth. Dr. David Reardon, who researches the aftereffects of abortion, summarized his study of women, all victims of sexual violence, and how they processed the question of abortion versus giving birth (parenting or placing for adoption). He summarized their attitude. "Giving birth, especially when conception was not desired, is a totally selfless act, a generous act, a display of courage, strength, and honor. It is proof that she is better than the rapist. While he was selfish, she can be generous. While he destroyed, she can nurture."[8] In other words, giving birth is a way of fighting back. That is healthy.

The divine command "You shall not murder" prohibits us from killing human beings to relieve pain or poverty or perceived suffering of any kind. We do not love the infirm or the deformed or the handicapped by killing them. Love does not kill; it shares in the burden that pain and suffering causes. That is the essence of compassion. We suffer with others and share our faith and strength and resources with them. There is never a justifiable reason to shed the blood of an innocent human being.[9]

2. Commit to not accepting the shedding of innocent blood by others. In Deuteronomy 21:1–9, God instructed His people how to respond to the shedding of innocent blood. It begins, "If in the land that the LORD your God is giving you to possess someone is found slain, lying in the open country, and it is not known who killed him, then your elders and your judges shall come out, and they shall measure the distance to the surrounding cities" (21:1–2). The distance to the body was to be measured to determine jurisdiction. The town that was closest was to take responsibility. This is in keeping with the principle that the closer you are, the more responsible you are. In other words, we are to love our neighbor.

Normal life was to be temporarily suspended. Business would have to suffer a bit. With great solemnity, the spiritual and judicial leaders were instructed to gather the people together and lead them through a costly ritual that would teach and reteach God's preeminent concern regarding the shedding of innocent blood.

> And the elders of the city that is nearest to the slain man shall take a heifer that has never been worked and that has not pulled in a yoke. And the elders of that city shall bring the heifer down to a valley with running water, which is neither plowed nor sown, and shall break the heifer's neck there in the valley. (Deut. 21:3–4)

For those of us in leadership roles in the church this passage ought to be especially instructive. Leaders must lead! The death of the innocent requires moral interpretation by its leaders, or people will accommodate themselves to it.

The lesson in this case is that the murder of this apparent stranger, whose death may not have affected anyone's life or routine, has nonetheless diminished them all, though they cannot see it. By taking people out of their routine and by requiring them to sacrifice a perfectly good, healthy (expensive) heifer and by having them sacrifice it on prime commercial real estate—land that has not been used up and that has running water on it—making it holy (unusable) space, the people would all feel the loss of life. They would feel in their wallets something of what God felt in His heart. The man might be a stranger to the town's people. He was not a stranger to God.

Whenever the innocent are killed in our midst, even if we do not know them, even if we could go right on about our business as if nothing has been lost, *something of value has been lost* and God wants us to feel it. And the occasion provides us an opportunity to recommit ourselves to the pro-life ethic.

In this case, the leaders were instructed to lead in public, corporate prayer.

> The priests, the sons of Levi, shall come forward . . . and they shall testify, "Our hands did not shed this blood, nor did our eyes see it shed. Accept

atonement, O Lᴏʀᴅ, for your people Israel, whom you have redeemed, and do not set the guilt of innocent blood in the midst of your people Israel, so that their blood guilt be atoned for." So you shall purge the guilt of innocent blood from your midst, when you do what is right in the sight of the Lᴏʀᴅ. (Deut. 21:5, 7–9)

In the first part of prayer, "Our hands did not shed this blood," the people reaffirm the negative law of God, "Do not murder" (Deut. 5:17). In the second part ("nor did our eyes see it shed"), they reaffirm the positive law, "love your neighbor as yourself" (Lev. 19:18). We are obligated not to shed innocent blood and we are obligated to prevent the shedding of innocent blood by others.

By leading the people through this costly process, and praying through the ethical obligations we bear toward one another, the hearts of the people become more sensitive to the value of human life. Without this, life in the community would go on as normal and the murder of this man would be processed as, "No big deal to me." What we do not grow sensitive to, we grow hard to.

Verse 9 concludes, "So you shall purge the guilt of innocent blood from your midst, when you do what is right in the sight of the Lᴏʀᴅ."

I take this to mean that for God's people, it is right and necessary at times to openly and corporately grieve the shedding of innocent blood and recommit our lives to holding each life precious. It means that it is right in God's sight that leaders lead God's people through a grieving and recommitment process regarding the shedding of innocent blood. And it is wrong if we do not.

With reference to abortion today, we are facing the death of the innocent in our midst. But they are unseen and unknown. So we feel no loss. This is the danger. Feeling no loss is the hardening of heart that comes naturally from making peace with death.

If you are a spiritual leader, and do not help your Christian community feel the loss of life in some way, to mourn it openly and use the occasion to call your people to cherish and defend human life, then you are helping them grow callous toward human life.

That is why I think there is value in having a Sanctity of Human Life Sunday on the calendar. It at least marks one time a year for pastors to lead well on this sensitive matter. It provides a church-wide opportunity to publicly address the shedding of innocent blood in the church and the neighborhood. It provides an occasion to reaffirm the will of God concerning human life. It even provides the opportunity for the people to feel economically what they cannot feel emotionally as they give and support their local pregnancy help center.

The Israelites were instructed to set aside some real estate—"a valley with a flowing spring"—for this very purpose. Pregnancy help centers are also places taken out of commercial use by the Christian community and dedicated to providing life-affirming assistance to women and couples in pregnancy distress. This proactive effort brings me to the third way to express the call of God.

3. Commit to personally rescuing the innocent where and whenever you can. In Luke 10:37, Jesus illustrates authentic love by pointing to the personal intervention of the Good Samaritan and calling us all to "go and do likewise."

Answering this call means obeying the law of love, or simply doing the mighty works that love prompts and compels us to do. This love comes from God and naturally flows toward our neighbor. Indeed, so absolute is the source and course of God's love that love for a neighbor is the proving ground for love for God. "If anyone . . . sees his brother in need yet closes his heart against him, how does God's love abide in him?" (1 John 3:17). It is not possible. To illustrate, Jesus told this parable:

> A man was going down from Jerusalem to Jericho, and he fell among robbers, who stripped him and beat him and departed, leaving him half dead. Now by chance a priest was going down that road, and when he saw him he passed by on the other side. So likewise a Levite, when he came to the place and saw him, passed by on the other side. But a Samaritan, as he journeyed, came to where he was, and when he saw

him, he had compassion. He went to him and bound up his wounds, pouring on oil and wine. Then he set him on his own animal and brought him to an inn and took care of him. And the next day he took out two denarii and gave them to the innkeeper, saying, "Take care of him, and whatever more you spend, I will repay you when I come back." (Luke 10:30–35)

Christ is illustrating the power of neighborly love that we possess when we possess the Spirit of Christ and love our Heavenly Father. It is a death-defying, lifesaving power. Love makes us see people as neighbors or brothers, not strangers or nonpersons. Love makes us willing to look at the plight of others, when self-interest prefers ignorance.

Love moves us to grieve and weep. But love is not satisfied with remorse alone. Love does not merely sorrow over death; it prompts intervention! It compels us to draw near to death rather than get distance from it. Love rushes into the breach like white corpuscles rush to a wound.

Love caused the Samaritan to act in a death-defying, lifesaving way. He *bandaged* the man's wounds, *put* him on a donkey, and *took* him to an inn. When the innkeeper asked, "And just who is going to pay for this?" love *paid* the bill. This is the power of neighborly love at work in us. This is Christianity in verbs.

In commanding us to "go and do likewise" (Luke 10:37), Jesus could just as easily have quoted

Scripture. He could have quoted Psalm 82:4, "Rescue the weak and the needy; deliver them from the hand of the wicked."

He could have quoted Proverbs 31:8–9, "Open your mouth for the mute, for the rights of all who are destitute. Open your mouth, judge righteously, defend the rights of the poor and needy."

Love will speak up for those who have no voice. Love will defend those who are being pressured and coerced by others. Love will rescue the innocent from those who would harm them. Of course, none of this could happen unless love also produces courage. But it does. Relying on God is also part of the call of God.

4. Commit to defending the innocent with faith toward God. God knows full well that there are times when defending innocent human life may cost us dearly. He commands us nonetheless. But He also supplies the faith and courage needed to carry it out.

Proverbs 24:10–12 says:

> If you faint in the day of adversity,
>   your strength is small.
> Rescue those who are being taken away to death;
>   hold back those who are stumbling to the
>   slaughter.
> If you say, "Behold, we did not know this,"
>   does not he who weighs the heart perceive it?
> Does not he who keeps watch over your soul
>   know it,
>   and will he not repay man according to his
>   work?

These "days of adversity" are serious and trying; innocents are being slaughtered. It might be state-sanctioned killing or the illegal action of a wicked individual or mob. No context is given for the command to "rescue those who are being taken away to death." If a specific context were described, we might limit application of the command to that group instead of applying the command *whenever any individual or group is dehumanized and killed to serve the purposes of others.* Difficult and costly as it may be, in such times we are commanded to actively oppose the slaughter of the innocent and to rescue them if possible.

In a strange way, we will know precisely when this passage from Proverbs is to be applied by the way we convince ourselves that it doesn't apply. Verse 12 says, "If you say, 'Behold, we did not know this,' does not he who weighs the heart perceive it?"

This verse takes direct aim at cowardice clothed as ignorance. When we are saying to ourselves, "I didn't know, I didn't realize, I had no idea," it is time to be honest. We sometimes prefer it that way. We do not want to know. Knowing makes us feel responsible for acting.

At the same time we all have an intuitive understanding that if we defend an innocent person who is under imminent attack, we shall not be treated any more kindly by his or her oppressor. If I see a man beating a woman and come to her aid, I am likely to get a beating too.

But notice how the call to rescue is written in such a way as to increase our confidence toward God and thus our courage. Verse 12 says, "Does not he who guards your life know it? Will he not repay each person according to what he has done?" (NIV). I do not take these words to be advocating some meritorious formula for salvation. We are saved by God's grace through faith in Jesus Christ, who died for our sins and was raised up by the same Spirit that now lives in us who believe.

So what is it saying? In times of trouble one's *faith* in God is demonstrated by the confidence and trust found in saying, "God is guarding my life." People with this kind of faith in God are free then to aid others—in this case, the weak and the innocent. Failure to do so means that our confession is proven shallow and empty ("If you faint in the day of adversity, your strength is small"!). Therefore, God will judge us faithless by our cowardly actions or faithful by our moral courage.

But entrust your life to His care and He will take take of you (now and forevermore). Believing this is what historically has given Christians the power to give of themselves so generously and to risk their lives when need be to save others.

One Christian said it this way, "If I profess with the loudest voice and the clearest exposition every portion of the truth of God except precisely that point which the world and the devil are at that moment attacking, I am not confessing Christ. Where the battle rages, there the loyalty of the soldier is proven, and to be steady on all the battle-fronts besides is mere flight and disgrace if he flinches at that point."[10]

In this postmodern culture, it is fairly easy to be a Christian, except when it comes to faithfully upholding God's lordship over matters of sexuality and life. We are flinching on that point. God calls us to entrust our lives and its well-being to Him. Through this faith, the courage to act on behalf of others is supplied.

Eva Fogalman, in her book *Conscience and Courage: Rescuers of Jews during the Holocaust,* gives us a glorious example of what "go and do likewise" means to those committed to following the law of love.

> In 1942, Wladyslaw Misiuna, a teenager from Radom, Poland, was recruited by the Germans to help inmates at the Fila Majdanek concentration camp start a rabbit farm to supply furs for soldiers at the Russian front. Wladyslaw felt responsible for the thirty young women he supervised. He stuffed his coat pockets with bread, milk, carrots, and pilfered potatoes and smuggled the food to them. But one day one of his workers, Devora Salzberg, contracted a mysterious infection. Wladyslaw was beside himself. He knew if the Germans discovered the open lesions on her arms they would kill her. Wladyslaw

knew that to save Devora he needed to cure her. But how? He took the simplest route. He infected himself with her blood and went to a doctor in town. The doctor prescribed a medication, which Wladyslaw then shared with Devora. Both were cured, and both survived the war.[11]

When I ask myself why is this story so satisfying, I think of several reasons. Misiuna chose good over evil. He demonstrated a clear commitment to cherish and defend innocent human life. He showed great moral courage. He was practical yet creative in his lifesaving plan. But the deepest reason that this story makes me rejoice is that it imitates the gospel of Jesus Christ. For "greater love has no one than this, that someone lay down his life for his friends" (John 15:13).

In contrast, consider another story from the same time. In *The Hiding Place*, Corrie ten Boom writes of the time when her family had taken in a young Jewish mother and her baby. When the local pastor came calling, Corrie put him to the test:

> "Would you be willing to take a Jewish mother and her baby into your home? They will almost certainly be arrested otherwise."

> Color drained from the man's face. He took a step back from me. "Miss Ten Boom! I do hope you're not involved with any of this illegal concealment and undercover business. It's just not safe! Think of your father! And your sister—she's never been strong!"

On impulse I told the pastor to wait and ran upstairs . . . I asked the mother's permission to borrow the infant. . . . Back in the dining room I pulled back the coverlet from the baby's face.

There was a long silence. The man bent forward, his hand in spite of himself reaching for the tiny fist curled round the blanket. For a moment I saw compassion and fear struggle in his face. Then he straightened. "No. Definitely not. We could lose our lives for that Jewish child!"

Unseen by either of us, Father had appeared in the doorway. "Give the child to me, Corrie," he said.

Father held the baby close, his white beard brushing its cheek . . . At last he looked up at the pastor. "You say we could lose our lives for this child. I would consider that the greatest honor that could come to my family."[12]

In one account we have a young teenage boy; in the other a trained and experienced pastor. Now which of these was the good neighbor? Which one answered the call? Which one glorified God?

============ CHAPTER EIGHT ============

Our Heritage and Our Legacy

Throughout history God's people have waged a war of love against all things that destroy body and soul. Beginning with the biblical record, we see a long and glorious record of people who cherished and defended innocent human life.

Reuben rescued Joseph from being killed by his own brothers (Gen. 37:21–22). The Hebrew midwives rescued baby boys from the infanticide of Pharaoh (Exod. 1:17). The soldiers of Saul rescued Jonathan from murder (1 Sam. 14:45). Obadiah rescued one hundred prophets from Jezebel and provided food and shelter for them (1 Kings 18:4). Esther risked her life to save her people from a royal (legalized) call for genocide (Esther 4:14; 7:3–4).

All these godly heroes understood the law of love. They understood the demands that love makes.

They did not shrink back in fear of the consequences that obedience to the law of love would bring.

Christianity from its very beginning has waged a fierce and steady battle against the ancient and unrelenting practices of paganism: abortion, infanticide, exposure, and abandonment of innocent babies.

The world into which Christianity was seeded saw nothing wrong with these crimes. In Rome, babies were abandoned outside the city walls to die from exposure or become food for wild beasts. Abortifacient concoctions, using herbs, pessaries, and poisons are well documented in Greek, Persian, Chinese, Arab, and Egyptian cultures. Infanticide was ritualized among Canaanite peoples; they burned babies in pyres as offerings to Molech. The historian George Grant says that not only were abortion, infanticide, exposure, and abandonment common throughout the cultures of the world at the time of Christ, but all the intellectuals of the day saw nothing wrong with it.

> None of the great minds of the ancient world—from Plato and Aristotle to Livy and Cicero, from Herodotus and Thucydides to Plutarch and Euripides—disparaged child-killing in any way. In fact, most of them actually recommended it.[1]

Then Christ came. And the Spirit that led Him to endure the cross in obedience and raised Him from the dead filled the hearts of His followers.

Immediately, Christians started to cherish and defend innocent human life.

Evidence for this arises in the very first generations of Christians. The *Didache* is one of the earliest documents we have from the Christian community. It was written about the same time that the Book of Revelation was written, around the end of the first century. Among its many instructions is a call to value the unborn child:

> There are two different ways: the way of life and the way of death, and the difference between these two ways is great. Therefore, do not murder a child by abortion or kill a newborn infant.[2]

Clement of Alexandria, Tertullian, Bishop Ambrose, Jerome—all key leaders of the early church—spoke out with vigor and consistency against the inhumanity of abortion and called on the church to stop it.

Augustine, Men, and Abortion

Augustine exposed the moral culpability that men bear in abortion. "They provoke women to such extravagant methods as to use poisonous drugs to secure barrenness; or else, if unsuccessful in this, to murder the unborn child."[3]

Men continue to be the number one reason that women choose abortion over giving birth. Men have their own reasons for favoring legal abortion. Consciously or unconsciously, abortion enables men to be more sexually promiscuous, since it allows them to deal with the dreaded complication of a baby. That is why early feminists such as Susan B. Anthony ardently opposed abortion as just another avenue for men to exploit women. "I deplore the horrible crime of child murder," she wrote, "but oh! thrice guilty is he who drove her to the desperation which impelled her."[4]

After talking to hundreds of women in pregnancy distress myself, and listening to many others who serve in pregnancy help centers, I can assure you that fathers, husbands, and boyfriends are pivotal in the abortion decision. Sociologist Dr. David Reardon, in his book *Aborted Women, Silent No More*, includes an account that I would say is typical based on my work in pregnancy help ministries.

> My family would not support my decision to keep the baby. My boyfriend said he would give me no emotional or financial help whatsoever. All the people that mattered told me to abort. When I said I didn't want to, they started listing reasons why I should. That it would have detrimental effects on my career, and my health, and that I would have no social life and no future with men. Could I actually do it alone? I started feeling like maybe I was crazy to want to keep it.
>
> I finally told everyone that I would have the abortion . . . I was scared to not do it because of how my

family and boyfriend felt. I'm so angry at myself for giving in to the pressure of others. I just felt so alone in my feelings to have my baby.[5]

According to Frederica Mathewes-Green in her book *Real Choices*, the highest number of women (38.2 percent) resort to abortion in response to pressure from a husband or a boyfriend.[6] David Reardon's research concluded, "The opinions and pressures of others played a major role in the final decision of most aborting women . . . nearly 55% of the respondents felt they had been very much 'forced' to abort by others."[7] Fifty-one percent of the time this other person was a husband or boyfriend.[8]

Dr. Phillip Ney, a Canadian researcher of abortion's psychological effects, reports that in a first pregnancy, if a woman's partner is present but not supportive, she has a four times greater chance of having an abortion; if the partner is absent, she has a six times greater chance of aborting. During a second pregnancy, if the partner is present but unsupportive, there is a 700 percent increased chance of abortion; and if the partner is absent, there is an 1800 percent increased chance of abortion.[9]

Given that abortion as a practice is actually a men's movement, rather than a women's movement, it is especially fitting that Christian men become part of the solution.

Basil of Caesarea, an Example of Pastoral Leadership

Basil of Caesarea (329–379), the great patri-archal hero of the Greek Orthodox wing of the church, was no doubt the greatest Christian leader of his age. A teacher and biblical scholar, he wrote tracts and books in defense of orthodox Christi-anity and against the heresy of his day, Arianism, which denied the full humanity of Jesus. A devoted and busy pastor in a large parish church, he held eighteen services a week (except for Christmas and Easter, when he led even more). He taught the youth, visited the sick, and kept up with heavy correspondence.

Basil was appalled to discover a guild of abor-tionists working in his city. He was also outraged. He was further horrified to learn that these abortion-ists were collecting fetal remains and selling them to cosmetologists in Egypt, who added them to various health and beauty creams they manufactured. All of this, including the abortion itself, was "legal."

Even worse, this was not something exceptional or rare in Roman culture. George Grant explains:

> According to the centuries old tradition of pater-familias, the birth of a Roman was not a biological fact. Infants were received into the world only as the family willed. A Roman did not have a child; he took a child. Immediately after birthing, if the family decided not to raise the child, he was simply

abandoned. There were special high places or walls outside most Roman cities where the newborn was taken and exposed to die.[10]

Basil responded to this inhumanity by providing pastoral leadership. He marshaled the resources of the Christian community to lifesaving and life-changing action.

He gave a series of sermons, using Scripture to affirm the sanctity of human life and the humanity of unborn children.

He called upon the Christian community to stop aborting their own babies, and he called them to actively defend innocent life by helping mothers in pregnancy distress find the help they needed to give life. In other words, he inspired the church to do the work and ministry of crisis pregnancy centers and maternity homes.

He launched a legislative battle using his power and influence to criminalize abortion.

He launched an education program to teach the entire city about the value of human life and to stigmatize and denounce abortion among the general population.

I cannot see how to improve upon this example in our own age. I can envision no appreciable success in delegitimizing and discarding abortion in our own age apart from our present-day leaders calling their churches to cherish and defend human life along the same avenues of action advocated by Basil.

The battle is not new; it is just our turn. In Basil, we have a great example to follow.

Emperor Valentinian, in response to Basil's work, criminalized the four evils of abortion, infanticide, exposure, and abandonment. In A.D. 374 he declared, "All parents must support their children conceived; those who brutalize or abandon them should be subject to the full penalty prescribed by law."[11]

"For the first time in human history," writes George Grant, "abortion, infanticide, exposure and abandonment were made illegitimate. The *sagae* were driven underground and eventually out of business altogether. The tradition of paterfamilias was all but overturned. The exposure walls were destroyed. And the high places were brought low. When Basil died just four years later, at the age of fifty, he had not only made his mark on the church, he had also altered the course of human history."[12]

Justinian and the Adoption Option

As Christian truths permeated the Western world, the pagan practices of abortion, infanticide, exposure, and abandonment continued to be denounced. In the sixth century Emperor Justinian (483–565) discovered that the laws protecting innocent life were contradictory and nonuniform.[13] He set out to codify the right to life.

His legislation prohibited abortion and protected the victims of harsh circumstances. Adoption was passionately encouraged. He declared:

> Those who expose children, possibly hoping they would die and those who use the potions of the abortionist are subject to the full penalty of the law. . . . Should exposure occur, the finder of the child is to see that he is baptized and that he is treated with Christian care and compassion. They may be adopted . . . even as we ourselves have been adopted into the kingdom of grace.[14]

Nothing seems more natural to me, as one welcomed into the family of God, than adoption. After all, besides the comparison to marriage, adoption is the most prominent point of comparison used to describe the glory of the gospel itself. Paul summarizes the gospel, saying, "Praise be to the God and Father of our Lord Jesus Christ, who . . . predestined us to be *adopted* as his sons through Jesus Christ" (Eph. 1:3, 5 NIV). The gospel is God's plan of *adoption*. The gospel is God taking us in as *His* children. "To all who received him, to those who believed in his name, he gave the right to become children of God" (John 1:12 NIV). No wonder Justinian, centuries ago, thought that adoption was the most natural of all Christian obligations.[15]

Sadly today, it is hard to adopt. There are few babies available. Here again is why pregnancy help ministries are so vital today. They are the last line of defense between the mother and baby and the abortionist and his curette. In the pregnancy help centers I worked with, most of the mothers either aborted or chose to parent. But those who placed for adoption were special indeed.[16]

The birth mother and the adoptive parents would come together. It is a place where many years of tearful longing are about to become a hope fulfilled. It is a place for the birth mother to give her child the life she cannot provide. It is an act of sacrificial love. Tears of sadness and tears of joy flow at the same time. Each is grateful for the other. Words are difficult to come by. The exchange is made and life wins out.

The Middle Ages and the Sanctity of Human Life Sunday

During the so-called Middle Ages, the church added the Feast of the Holy Innocents to its liturgical calendar. Matthew 2:16 tells of Herod's anger over the birth of Christ. Hoping to eliminate this "threat" to his kingdom, Herod ordered the slaughter of all the boys in Bethlehem and the surrounding area who were two years old or younger. The wrenching grief of their mothers had been prophesied—"Rachael weeping for her children; she refused to be comforted, because they are no more" (Matt. 2:18; see Jer. 31:15).

By appointing the Feast of the Holy Innocents, the church sought to make sure that her leaders had occasion to remind the people to cherish and defend innocent human life.

Today, in both liturgical and nonliturgical churches, there is a growing practice of designating the third Sunday in January as Sanctity of Human Life Sunday. The date was chosen in solemn recognition that on January 22, 1973, the US Supreme Court ruled that the unborn child did not have equal constitutional protection. In the first generation of legal abortion, an estimated 55,772,015 unborn children have died as a result of this decision.[17] Admittedly, numbers do not move us much. But the observance of a nationwide Sanctity of Human Life Sunday does provide a place holder for pastors and leaders to proclaim the gospel of life.

The Reformation and the Call to Rescue the Innocent

John Calvin (1509–1564), the leader of the Swiss Reformation, was passionate about defending innocent human life:

> The unborn child . . . though enclosed in the womb of its mother, is already a human being . . . and should not be robbed of the life which it has not yet begun to enjoy. If it seems more horrible to kill a man in his own house than in a field, because a

man's house is his place of most secure refuge, it
ought surely to be deemed more atrocious to destroy an unborn child in the womb before it has
come to light.[18]

He called on the church to be as diligent and
devoted to the preservation of the innocent as they
were to the preservation and dissemination of the
gospel message to the guilty. He called them to suffer for both, if need be.

> I say that not only they that labor for the defense of
> the gospel, but they that in any way maintain the
> cause of righteousness, suffer persecution for righ-
> teousness. Therefore, whether declaring God's truth
> against Satan's falsehoods or in taking up the protec-
> tion of the good and innocent against the wrongs of
> the wicked, we must undergo the offenses and hatred
> of the world, which may imperil either our life, our
> fortunes or our honor.[19]

Meanwhile, Ignatius of Loyola (1491–1556) was
one of the most prominent leaders of the Catholic
Reformation during the same time that Calvin was
calling for reforms. He called the church to face the
truth of abortion squarely and to resolve to do something about it.

> Life is God's most precious gift. Abortion . . . is not
> merely an awful tyranny, it is a smear against the
> integrity of God as well. Suffer as we must, even die
> if need be, such rebellion against heaven must not
> be free to run its terrible courses.[20]

Vincent de Paul's Reminder that Answering God's Call Is Joy

In Paris, the pastor Vincent de Paul (1581–1660) led his church to demonstrate their commitment to holding each life precious by launching special ministries to help galley slaves, abandoned elderly, unwanted children, and convicts. In 1652, de Paul learned of a guild of abortionists operating in the slums of Paris. Vincent took to his pulpit to sound a clear trumpet on the demands made on those who claimed to follow the law of love.

He reminded the people that pro-life work was mandatory; the church is commanded to rescue the innocent. He also reminded them that God's commands are not burdensome; rather, they are profoundly fulfilling:

> Whene'er God's people gather, there is life in the midst of them—yea, Christ's gift to us as a people is life, and that more abundantly. To protect the least of these, our brethren is not merely facultative [a choice], it is exigent [urgent]. In addition though, it is among the greatest and most satisfying of our sundry stewardships.[21]

Missions and the Innocent

Kenneth Scott Latourette, the famous church historian, called the nineteenth century the Glorious

Century. For Protestants, it is the age of modern missions. The father of this movement is William Carey (1761–1834). He is famous for his creed, "Expect great things from God, attempt great things for God."

Raised as a shoe cobbler, Carey left England to bring the gospel to India. He spent forty years there. Modern India owes much to the passion, humility, innovation, and commitment to life that Carey brought with him.

Vishal and Ruth Mangalwadi, in their book *The Legacy of William Carey*, outline the remarkable contributions he made to modern India.[22] They point out that Carey was a botanist. One of three varieties of eucalyptus found only in India is named after him: *Careya Herbacea*. According to Carey's gospel, all of creation is good and points to the glory of God. He published the first books on natural history in India to stress that "all thy works praise thee, O Lord."

Carey was an industrialist. He helped introduce the steam engine to India and was the first to produce indigenous paper for printing and publishing books.

Carey was an economist. Believing that God hated usury, and seeing the pervasive and impoverishing effects of loans with interest rates from 36 to 72 percent, Carey introduced the idea of savings banks to India.

Carey was a publisher. He brought the modern science of printing and publishing to India. He established the first newspaper ever printed in any Oriental language, because according to Carey's gospel, "Above all forms of truth and faith, Christianity seeks free discussion."

Carey was an astronomer. He introduced the science and mathematics of astronomy to India. Since God created the world and set men to rule it, heavenly bodies were not deities. They could be measured, charted, and counted. The science of astronomy, Carey recognized, would topple the fatalism and superstitious fear sown by astrology.

Carey was a translator and educator. He started dozens of schools for Indian children of all castes. He started the first college in Asia, at Serampore near Calcutta. He rose to become a professor of languages.

Above all, Carey was a missionary. His desire was to bring the gospel to the people. He started by translating the Bible into Bengali, Sanskrit, and Marathi. He wrote two grammars and a dictionary. After nineteen years of work, a fire struck and all these manuscripts were destroyed. Carey bowed before Almighty God and started all over again.

By the end of his life, he had translated and published the Bible or parts of it into thirty-six languages and dialects, started schools and hospitals, founded Serampore College, and opened numerous medical clinics.

But the same gospel that led him to do all this never allowed him to be silent when innocent blood was being shed. He saw missionary work as both preaching salvation and defending the weak. The law of love compelled both.

Upon arriving in India he learned that abortion, infanticide, exposure, and abandonment were part of the way of life. One day he "came across a basket suspended from a tree. Inside were the remains of an infant which had been exposed; only the skull was left, the rest having been devoured by white ants."[23] When he moved to Serampore, he discovered that more than 100 babies were "sacrificed" every year, thrown into the Ganges River, where they were eaten by alligators. "This was looked upon as a most holy sacrifice—giving the Mother Ganges the fruit of their bodies for the sons of their souls."[24]

Carey launched an all-out effort to stop this ritual of child sacrifice. He was accused of imposing his moral values on others. Yet this practice was eventually outlawed. And the pro-life legislation that was eventually passed is called to this very day "Carey's Edict."[25]

One hundred years later, the missionary Amy Carmichael (1867–1951) arrived in southern India. She learned that "the sale of children as temple prostitutes to be 'married to the gods' and then made available to Hindu men who frequented the temple was one of the 'secret sins' of Hinduism."[26] When a seven-year-old girl ran away from such a cult temple, Amy, following the law of love, took her in and refused to return her. In defending this innocent life, Amy offended the acceptable, legal practices of her time. Nonetheless, her actions declared, "Not on my watch!"

For refusing to accept the destruction of innocent life, she was harshly criticized by the government. She was even charged with kidnapping on several occasions! In her own words, saving this one innocent child "created an enormous fuss."[27] But she continued to rescue the innocent, and twelve years later, she had 139 young girls under her care.

The historian Ruth Tucker adds:

> The children were educated and physically cared for, special attention was paid to the development of their "Christian character." To critics who charged that her emphasis on physical needs, education and character-building was not evangelistic enough, Amy responded: ". . . one cannot save and then pitchfork souls into heaven . . . Souls are more or less securely fastened to bodies . . . and as you cannot get the souls out and deal with them separately, you have to take them both together."[28]

Her main mission was the gospel, which is aimed at the guilty. But she cared for the innocent as the situation demanded. In the end, both causes advanced.

Harriet Tubman, Saving One Life at a Time

Harriet Tubman (1820–1913) orchestrated the rescue of hundreds of runaway slaves out of her home in Philadelphia through the Underground Railroad. She and other abolitionists recognized that they could not change the laws, but they could rescue slaves one person and family at a time.

The historical parallels to the present situation are remarkable. Abortion and slavery both required a Supreme Court decision. The Dred Scott case (1857) ruled that blacks were not persons worthy of protection under the Constitution. *Roe v. Wade* (1973) ruled the same for unborn children. The slave, like the unborn child, was considered private property. Slavery was defended as a matter of choice: "If you don't believe in slavery, don't own any." So today, advocates of legal abortion argue, "If you don't like abortion, don't have one."

As we move past the fortieth anniversary of legal abortion in 2013, we know that the legislative and constitutional struggle will continue for the foreseeable future.

While we wait for God in His sovereignty to pierce the conscience of America and recognize the inherent right to life of the unborn child, we must continue to rescue babies, one mother and couple at a time. One mother at a time, as neighbors helping neighbors, following the model of the pregnancy help movement as it was birthed a generation ago and continues to expand from cities and states across the country to a worldwide mission.

Heartbeat International and Carenet are two leadership organizations that have trained Christian communities to establish pregnancy help centers and maternity homes.[29] Heartbeat has more than one thousand affiliated pregnancy help ministries. They estimate that about two thousand babies a week are rescued from abortion, through their affiliates. This happens one woman at a time.

In 1991, after nearly twenty years of legal abortion in the United States, there were 2,176 independent abortion businesses operating across the country. But during these two decades Christians and churches worked together to establish more than seven hundred pregnancy help centers. Today, there are more than four thousand pregnancy help centers in the United States and fewer than 650 abortion businesses.[30]

Newton, Wilberforce, and the Gospel of Life

In England the slave trade, fully legal and institutionalized, came under increased attack from pulpits to the Parliament. Lord Melbourne decried the rising voices of pastors who preached the sanctity of human life and decried the inhumanity of slavery. "Things have come to a pretty pass when religion is allowed to invade public life."[31]

Reverend John Newton was one of the people he probably had in mind. Newton was a former captain of a "slaver" ship. He knew better than anyone the inhumanity of the slave trade. After his conversion, he left that "business" and made his way into the Anglican Church as a preacher. He was a living example that God loves the guilty and is willing to forgive the repentant. His hymn "Amazing Grace" is the most popular hymn in church history.

But Newton also knew that God loved the innocent as well, and he took God's call from Proverbs 31:9. "Open your mouth, judge righteously, defend the rights of the poor and needy." He wrote a pamphlet exposing the vile inhumanity of the slave trade. He testified before legislators. He taught from the Scriptures the sanctity of all human life.

One man who heard him was William Wilberforce. As a member of Parliament, Wilberforce labored for twenty years to abolish the slave trade (1787–1807). Having succeeded, he labored another twenty-six years to abolish slavery itself. On July 26, 1833, slavery was outlawed in Britain and human rights for blacks were secured. Three days later Wilberforce died.

In a remarkable historic parallel, God has transformed most of the key leaders that led to the legalization of abortion in America. Bernard Nathanson, mentioned earlier as the abortionist who helped plan the legal effort to legalize abortion nationwide, came to faith in Christ in 1996. Like Newton, Nathanson, in his book *The Hand of God*, writes of his amazement at the grace of God who can forgive "sinners." During the last half of his life, Nathanson wrote and spoke with a painful eloquence until he died in 2011, calling the nation to wholly reject what he had once championed.

Norma McCorvey is the "Jane Roe" of the infamous *Roe v. Wade* Supreme Court decision. To cover up an affair in 1969, Norma lied about her pregnancy, saying she was raped. Two feminist lawyers recruited her to become America's test case on abortion. She herself never had an abortion, but her case nullified all restrictions on abortion in America.

In 1995, Operation Rescue, the group that organized nonviolent sit-ins outside abortion facilities, opened an office next door to the abortion clinic where Norma was employed. Several encounters outside their offices during lunch hour softened her heart. When eight-year-old Emily Mackey, the daughter of a pro-life volunteer, asked Norma to attend church with her, she agreed. That night she gave her life to Christ. She was baptized later that year. The *New York Post* headline said, "Jane Roe Flip-Flops on Abortion" and underneath screamed, "I'M PRO-LIFE."[32]

If we follow the law of love, one day, as a nation, we will look back on abortion the way we currently look back on slavery. As we courageously speak up

and wisely direct God's people toward compassionate intervention, we should go forward recalling the
timeless words of William Wilberforce:

> Never, never will we desist till we . . . extinguish
> every trace of this bloody traffic, of which our poster-
> ity, looking back to the history of these enlightened
> times, will scarce believe that it has been suffered
> to exist so long a disgrace and dishonor to this
> country.[33]

CHAPTER NINE

Whatever Happened to . . .

*T*he young, sweet-voiced sixteen-year-old who called my office (see chapter 2), so immobilized by fear of pregnancy that she threatened suicide and so clear about the evil of taking a human life that she would never be able to live with herself afterward, never came into our center. I never heard from her again and do not know what happened to her. God used this young woman to fix my mind and heart on the urgency of God's calling. I doubt I changed her life. But she changed mine.

The couple who came in with nine of their ten children in tow had a happier ending. While the rambunctious children tore the office apart, we adults talked through the abortion question. At one point I asked the father to consider the following: "If money is the issue, and you cannot afford eleven children, why not kill your fifteen-year-old and save the fifteen-week-old unborn child? You will save much more money. After all, teenagers eat more, they want two-hundred sneakers and a college degree." He translated this proposed solution to his wife. Then he said nervously, "We can't do that." I agreed, then underscored the point of my proposal, "No matter what financial problems we face, killing our children is not a solution." He replied, "Of course you are right." He told his wife that abortion is not the answer. She began to cry with joy!

This immigrant mother would have been devastated by an abortion. Her lifelong mission was raising her children. Providentially, a local church had held a "diaper drive," where everyone comes to church with a package of diapers to give away to new mothers. Church members had delivered several huge plastic bags filled with dozens of such packages to our office. I gave them all to this family of ten, with one on the way.

"This is a down payment," I told them, "on the promise that those who trust in God will not go hungry."

In the weeks that followed, Christians in their hometown offered this father work. They assisted the family with baby clothes and other necessities. Some months later they returned with their baby. It is tough to raise ten kids; but it is not measurably tougher raising eleven. Things work out.

A graduate student went on to have her baby. The father, who threatened my life because I was "ruining his life," came to see that, indeed, having a baby and becoming a father was a great blessing. He became very excited about the baby. When we prepared a layette of goods for them (which pregnancy help centers typically provide to new mothers), she came by to pick it up and to thank us. I was hoping to greet the father, but the mother said that he was too embarrassed by his past behavior to come and see me. I sent word that I was happy for him and would welcome a visit anytime.

The daughters of the three local pastors also decided to have their babies. Two of them married. One of them, deeply hurt by her father's initial outrage, worked out her disappointment with her father. He worked out his disappointment with his daughter. They figured out what the law of love demanded of them both, and when her son was born, she named him after her father.

What happened to "X", the one who was a senior at a local Christian college? She was about to abort her faith as well as her baby. She had been told by the abortion facility that she was fourteen weeks pregnant. The cost of her abortion was high. She called our center, looking for a better price. She ended up kneeling and recommitting her life to Jesus Christ in our counseling room. She decided to trust that God could forgive her and that God would take care of her and her baby. We paid for her initial prenatal care visit. The day after, the doctor called and asked me if I was sitting down. I sat down and the doctor said, "She isn't pregnant!"

This beautiful young woman had gone into the abortion facility in a state of panic. She was racked with guilt over behavior she did not believe was proper. They sold her an abortion and scheduled an appointment for her to return once she found the money. Had she not come to my office, she never would have known that she wasn't even pregnant. Her story is one reason many pregnancy help centers now typically offer ultrasound verification.

For the couple who came in, admitting a back-ground of drugs and alcoholism, unemployed and both married to someone else, it was a difficult case. The baby arrived and, eventually, with the help of many Christians doing a small part to help, they made it through several years of instability.

Some mothers go on to place their child for adoption. Some marry. Some learn from their mis-takes, and others repeat them again and again. In each case, we ask ourselves, what does love require of us in this situation? Then we seek to follow that course, simply and directly, with the aid of the Christian community.

CHAPTER TEN

Final Encouragements

*U*nless your local church consists only of very old people and lacks any evangelistic thrust, you have men and women in your church who are struggling with the bloodguilt of abortion. In mine it turned out to be about 30 percent. And we know that one-third of all American women will suffer at least one abortion by the age of forty-five. As the testimonies of women and couples reveal, this sin so stains the conscience that many struggle with whether God can or should forgive them.

Bring Their Consciences to the Cross

If you are a pastor in the care of souls and hope to see your people grow strong, change their neighborhood, and move out into this troubled world with confidence, please recognize that abortion, and the bloodguilt it invokes, must be dealt with. It needs to be called out by name, confessed by name, and brought under a gospel that declares that there is no forgiveness for the shedding of innocent blood except by the shedding of innocent blood, that is, by the blood of Christ.[1] That is where atonement is experienced as the cleansing of one's conscience and a fresh start.

Silence is not atonement. Silence in the pulpit is not interpreted as compassionate caution on your part. It is understood to mean that this sin is so horrific that you cannot mention it. Satan, who accuses believers day and night, fills in this silence with relentless condemnation (Rev. 12:10).

Preach All That God Says

Perversely, for those who are frightened and embarrassed by pregnancy, silence is interpreted to mean approval of abortion. The tempter here whispers approval, "If abortion was really the killing of a child, surely the pastor would say something about it. He never has so it must be no big deal." Do not be ignorant of his schemes. Your people are in danger and you are there to protect them. Your weapon is largely the Word of God and the glory of preaching. Your primary pro-life work is to preach the word and model the grace of God. But in saying that, I appeal to you to preach all that God says, including the Scripture examined throughout this book.

Uphold God's Radical Vision for Marriage and Sexuality

Abortion and all its guilt and trauma is largely the bitter fruit of sexual immorality. Anyone who cares about ending abortion will soon trace it back to this deeper problem. Pregnancy help centers intervene in the moments of crises, but they all eventually work back toward the problem of sexual choices. Teaching sexual integrity—upholding the biblical vision and promised joy of marital sexual intimacy—is powerful pro-life work.[2] I encourage you to make sure your church is routinely present-ing this biblical alternative to the meet-up, hook-up, and break-up standard of our popular culture.

Hold True, but Link Arms

I am Reformed and evangelical in my theologi-cal convictions and happily so. But I recognize that ending abortion will take concerted and cooperative labor with those outside my circle. Without com-promising your theological convictions, perhaps even as "collaborating co-belligerents" as Scott Klusendorf calls them, summon your people to work with other churches (Catholics, evangelicals, charismatics, fundamentalists, etc.) in rescuing the women and couples in your town who are in the cross-hairs of abortion.[3]

From One Generation to the Next

During the past forty years, priests and pastors across the land have helped birth a vibrant, multi-dimensional, modern pro-life movement. Chuck Swindoll has been a pastoral leader during this time. He wrote:

> Of all the issues I have encountered through all the years I have been engaged in people-related involve-ments, none are more significant than the sanctity of life and sexual purity. The groundswell of concern surrounding each has made them the inescapable is-sues of our times.[4]

If this has been true of those who came of age with the Beatles, it is still true of those who came of age with the iPhone. If you are of the first genera-tion, get the baton, the gospel of life, into in the hands of the second. If you are in the second, grab hold of it and run.

Let me know if I can help.[5] Together, may we see the fragrance of Christ emanate from us as the very aroma of life itself.

Notes

Preface to the Second Edition

1. See Rodney Stark, *For the Glory of God: How Monotheism Led to Reformations, Science, Witch-Hunts and the End of Slavery* (Princeton, NJ: Princeton University Press, 2003).

2. Quoted in Charles Colson, *Kingdoms in Conflict* (Grand Rapids: Zondervan, 1987), 102.

Chapter 1: The Aroma of Life

1. Quoted in a *Focus on the Family* radio spot produced for pregnancy help centers.

Chapter 2: The Great Test

1. Eric Metaxas, *Bonhoeffer: Pastor, Martyr, Prophet, Spy* (Nashville: Thomas Nelson, 2010), 393.

2. Pope John Paul II, *The Gospel of Life* (New York: Random House, 1995), 4, 22.

3. I am not a prophet. But it would not be unjust if my generation, the baby boomers, who demanded the

right to get rid of unwanted and costly children at hospitals and clinics were the first generation to be taken to end-of-life hospital wards and termination centers set up for similar reasons. We reap what we sow.

4. Peter Singer, "Taking Human Life," in *Practical Ethics* 2nd ed. (New York: Cambridge University Press, 1993). Singer is not alone. Francis Crick and James Watson, who won a Nobel Prize for the discovery of the double-helix structure of DNA, advocate that all newborns who fail a health test be euthanized (see C. Everett Koop, "Life and Death and the Handicapped Unborn," *Issues in Law and Medicine* 5, no. 1 [June 22, 1989], 101). Steven Pinker of MIT, asserting that humans are ever evolving, calls for acceptance of "neonaticide" as natural selection in process (see Steven Pinker, "Why They Kill Their Newborns," *New York Times*, November 2, 1997).

5. Peter Singer, FAQ at http://www.princeton.edu/~psinger/faq.html as of February 5, 2012.

6. Alberto Giubilini and Francesca Minerva, "After-birth Abortion: Why Should the Baby Live?" *Journal of Medical Ethics*, February 23, 2012, http://jme.bmj.com/content/early/2012/04/12/medethics-2011-100411.full?sid=a8c538f6-f62f-43c3-b544-ac5232031ed0.

7. See Mary C. Curtis, "'After-birth Abortion': Can They Be Serious?" Washington Post blog, March 5, 2012, http://www.washingtonpost.com/blogs/she-the-people/post/after-birth-abortion-can-they-be-%20serious/2012/03/03/gIQADgiOsR_blog.html.

8. I think of David Platt as one example. He is the pastor of the Church at Brook Hills, a mega-church in Birmingham, Al. He is also the author of *Radical* which has sold more than1 million copies and contrasts living for the American Dream versus living for the gospel. To see him lead well, both sensitivity and clarity, on abortion, see

his sermon "The Child Yet Unborn," July 3, 2011, http://www.brookhills.org/serving/abortionandthechurch.html.

9. Numerous peer-reviewed medical studies have found an association between abortion and suicide. For example, a 2005 study by Mika Gissler in the *European Journal of Public Health* found that abortion was associated with a six-times-higher risk for suicide compared to birth. And a 2010 study by Natalie P. Mota in the *Canadian Journal of Psychiatry* found that "abortion was associated with an increased likelihood of several mental disorders—mood disorders . . . substance abuse disorders . . . as well as suicidal ideation and suicide attempts." Clarke Forsythe and Marilee Smith, "Disclosing the Abortion-Suicide Association," *Washington Times,* http://www.washingtontimes.com/news/2012/feb/20/disclosing-the-abortion-suicide-association/?page=all.

As a result, some states are passing laws requiring "a suicide advisory" be issued by abortion providers/businesses to give patient/women "a description of all known medical risks of the procedure and statistically significant risk factors . . . including . . . depression [and] increased risk of suicide ideation and suicide." Of course the abortion industry is opposing it. The statute is currently being litigated under *Planned Parenthood v. Rounds*.

Chapter 3: Knowing the Times

1. For a comprehensive overview of the 1973 Roe v. Wade and Doe v. Bolton rulings, plus the story of the people involved, see http://www.endroe.org/roeanalysis.aspx.

2. Guttmacher Institute, "Facts on Induced Abortion Worldwide," February 2011, http:// www.guttmacher.org/pubs/fb_IAW.html.

3. Guttmacher Institute, Facts on Induced Abortion in the United States, August 2011, http://www.guttmacher.org/pubs/bf_induced_abortion.html.

4. David Reardon, *Aborted Women, Silent No More* (Chicago: Loyola University Press, 1997), xi.

5. For a full treatment of abortion sequelae, see David Reardon, *Aborted Women, Silent No More.* Or http://afterabortion.org/.

6. Guttmacher Institute, "Facts on Induced Abortion in the United States." August 2011, http://www.guttmacher.org/pubs/bf_induced_abortion.html.

7. I wrote more about this in *The Great Work of Gospel: How We Experience God's Grace* (Wheaton, IL: Crossway, 2006).

8. Carol Everett, "Selling Teen Abortions." Available from Arizona Right to Life, http://azrtl.org/index.php/get-educated/literature-media-library/.

9. Guttmacher Institute,, "Facts on Induced Abortion in the United States," August 2011, http://www.guttmacher.org/pubs/bf_induced_abortion.html.

10. Centers for Disease Control and Prevention, "Abortion Surveillance—United States, 2008," *Morbidity and Mortality Weekly Report*, Surveillance Summaries, November 25, 2011, http://www.cdc.gov/mmwr/preview/mmwrhtml/ss6015a1.htm.

11. Interestingly, National Abortion Federation interprets this as evidence that woman are not using abortion as birth control. See http://www.prochoice.org/pubs_research/publications/downloads/about_abortion/women_who_have_abortions.pdf.

12. Guttmacher Institute, "The Limitations of U.S. Statistics on Abortion, January 1997, http://www.guttmacher.org/pubs/ib14.html.

13. Abby Johnson Op-Ed in The Hill, "Exposing the Planned Parenthood Business Model," April 4, 2011, http://thehill.com/blogs/congress-blog/politics/153699-exposing-the-planned-parenthood-business-model.

14. Chiaroscuro Foundation Report, "Does Planned Parenthood Need or Deserve Federal Funds?," March 2011, Susan B. Anthony List, http://www.sba-list.org/sites/default/files/content/shared/Chiaroscuro_PP_Analysis_March_2011.pdf.

15. "Abortion Attitudes in the African American Community," Center for Business and Economic Research (University of Dayton). The research was commissioned by Dayton Right to Life. For analysis, see http://afterabortion.org/2001/the-awakening-of-african-americans/.

16. Guttenmacher Institute, "Facts on Induced Abortion in the United States," August 2011, http://www.guttmacher.org/pubs/bf_induced_abortion.html.

17. "Summary of Vital Statistics, New York City, 2009, The City of New York" http://www.nyc.gov/html/doh/downloads/pdf/vs/2009sum.pdf.

18. See http://blackgenocide.org/home.html.

19. *Lifelines*, A Special Report of Heartbeat International, Spring 2011, 2.

Chapter 4: God's Passion for Life

1. I am carrying over here, what I also wrote in *Innocent Blood: Challenging the Powers of Death with the Gospel of Life* (Adelphi, MD: Cruciform Press, 2011), 28–29.

2. George Grant, *Third Time Around: The History of the Pro-Life Movement from the First Century to the Present* (Brentwood, TN: Wolgemuth & Hyatt, 1991), 15.

3. Grant, 15.

4. When the Bible speaks of "innocent blood" or simply, the "innocent" it is not referring to innocence before God. No one is innocent in that sense. Rather, it refers to being innocent in relationship to others, innocent before the laws that govern our actions toward each other. If I am falsely accused of stealing your wallet, you will hear me shout smartly, "I am innocent!"

5. John Jefferson Davis, *Abortion and the Christian* (Phillipsburg, NJ: Presbyterian & Reformed, 1984), 40.

6. Clifford Bajema, *Abortion and the Meaning of Personhood* (Grand Rapids: Baker Book House, 1974), 32.

7. In common parlance one is pregnant from conception (fertilization) to birth. In the medical world, pregnancy-related terms are in debate. Some medical dictionaries now define pregnancy as beginning at implantation rather than conception. But this is misleading, and in my view, intentionally misleading.

In 2004, the American Medical Association passed a resolution in favor of making "Plan B" emergency contraception available over-the-counter. One of the claims in the resolution was that hormonal contraception that may affect implantation "cannot terminate an established pregnancy." To the layperson using the pill and concerned about not destroying human life, that sounds like a comfort, because he or she equates fertilization with being pregnant. But by "established pregnancy" they mean the pill will not harm a newly conceived human being after it has implanted in the uterus and begins to draw in nourishment. But before that, the pill is chemically designed under its "third mechanism" to prevent a newly conceived human being from implanting in the uterus. It is thus expelled (aborted). For a full discussion of this medical debate over terminology and the three mechanisms at work in all birth control pills available in the U.S., see Randy Alcorn, *Does the Birth Control Pill Cause Abortions?* 10th ed. (Sandy, OR: EPM Ministries, 2011).

According to the timeline in Luke, when Mary was greeted by Elizabeth, Mary was in the earliest stages of pregnancy, by which I mean she was carrying the fertilized egg that was the human being, Jesus Christ, although He may well still have been traveling down the fallopian tube and not yet implanted in Mary's womb. We do not know for sure because we do not know the time and distance it took her to arrive.

Chapter 5: Healing for the Morally Blind

1. Cited in Scott Klusendorf, *The Case for Life* (Wheaton, IL: Crossway, 2009), 35.

2. Scott Klusendorf clarifies each of these qualities to help us understand why it is not accurate to say that an embryo is a mere clump of cells. Klusendorf writes, "To say the embryo is *distinct* means it is different in kind from any cell of its parents. Sperm and egg, for example, cease to exist at fertilization, their role being restricted to surrendering their constituents into the makeup of a new entity, the embryo . . . Most importantly, the embryo is a complete or whole human organism rather than part of another entity. All of its cells work together in tandem toward the growth of a single entity, the embryo." *(The Case for Life, 37–38.)*

3. Keith Moore and T.V.N. Persaud, *The Developing Human: Clinically Oriented Embryology,* 8th ed. (Philadelphia: Saunders/Elsevier, 2008), 15. Cited in Klusendorf, *The Case for Life,* 35.

4. These fetal development milestones come from Keith L. Moore and T.V.N. Persaud, *The Developing Human*, 5th ed. (Philadelphia: W.B. Saunders, 1993).

5. Calculated from data provided by the Guttmacher Institute and the Centers for Disease Control, "Abortion Surveillance, 2008," *Morbidity and Mortality Weekly Report*, Surveillance Summaries, November 25, 2011, http://www.cdc.gov/mmwr/preview/mmwrhtml/ss6015a1.htm#Tab7.

6. Roe v. Wade declares that the state may limit late-term abortions in the interest of protecting fetal life after viability, "except when it is necessary to preserve the life or health of the mother." Doe v. Bolton, the Supreme Court decision handed down with Roe v. Wade, defined the health of the mother to be "the physical, emotional, psychological, familial and the woman's age . . . all these factors may relate to health."

The U.S. Senate Judiciary Committee concluded in an official report (Report #98-149) after extensive hearings in 1982: "No significant legal barriers of any kind whatsoever exist today in the United States for a woman to obtain an abortion for any reason during any stage of her pregnancy."

7. "Q & A with Bernard Nathanson," *Focus on the Family Citizen* magazine, August 26, 1996, 7.

8. Bernard Nathanson, *The Hand of God* (Washington, DC: Regnery, 1996), 19.

9. See "Maternal Bonding in Early Fetal Ultrasound," *New England Journal of Medicine*, February 17, 1983.

10. We have already shown that this is not the way the Bible views human beings. But we must be prepared to make the rational and philosophical defense as well.

11. John Ensor and Scott Klusendorf, *Students for Life* (Peabody, MA: Hendrickson, 2012).

12. Sir Charles Bell, *The Hand: Its Mechanism and Vital Endowments as Evincing Design*, 4th ed. (London: William Pickering, 1834).

Chapter 6: The Injustice of Abortion

1. See Alvin Schmidt's excellent book, *How Christianity Changed the World* (Grand Rapids: Zondervan, 2004).

2. As a practical matter, one of the things I find so deeply satisfying about pregnancy help ministries and helping mothers and couples escape the violence of abortion, is that I am automatically engaged in the chronic ills of poverty, fatherlessness and more—things I do sincerely care about.

3. The same has been true of other forms of mass killing. Our vocabulary is simply not up to the challenge of conveying the evil. Nor are we able to process and register the evil after a certain point. We cannot imagine such evil and therefore we resist believing the reports at first. The powers that drive this evil, it seems to me, rely on this human psychological self-defense mechanism. They know that the worse the evil is, the more we will deny it or reduce it. Then the trap is set.

4. Bernard Nathanson, "Pro-Choice 1990," *New Dimensions*, October 1990, 38.

5. Kim Flodin, "Why I Don't March," My Turn, *Newsweek*, February 12, 1990, 8.

6. I am indebted to John Piper, Preaching Pastor at Bethlehem Baptist Church in Minneapolis for first pointing this out to me. See "Where Does Child Killing Come From?" Sermon from January 25, 1998, http://www .desiringgod.org/resource-library/sermons/where-does-child-killing-come-from.

7. Reports of human bondage, torture, mass murder and other atrocities must be documented and viewed in order for people of good will to believe it and to arouse themselves to action. The same is true with abortion, and I would add, especially true. Millions of people have rationalized their abortion activities. Pictures, not words, are needed for the truth of abortion to penetrate those defenses. Until we see the pictures, we will not believe the severity of the evil and injustice in the practice. The Center for Bio-Ethic Reform has documented abortion surgery and its aftermath. This documentation can be seen at http://www.abortionno.org/. They ask correctly, "If the *pictures* of abortion are too much to view, what does that say about the *practice* of abortion?"

Chapter 7: Commitments That Answer the Call

1. Pope John Paul II, *The Gospel of Life, Evangelism Vitae* (New York: Random House, 1995), 70.

2. Virginia Ramey Mollenkott, "Reproductive Choice: Basic to Justice for Women," *Christian Scholar's Review* 17 (March 1988), 291.

3. If a law was proposed that justified "professor-cide," the killing of professors, my guess is that Professor Mollenkott would not fall for the "silence equals permission" idea. I notice that those who find philosophical justification for devaluing other groups of human beings always have in their sights weak and defenseless ones, who cannot fight back—babies, the mentally disabled, the handicapped, the elderly at a certain point. It is never twenty-two-year-old marines. Eugenicists never chose their own race for downsizing, if not genocide. The

justifications are always aimed at others who are politically disenfranchised—powerless before the state.

4. This is the way Scott Klusendorf helps us get back to the main question of abortion: what is it? If it is human, there is no justifiable circumstance in which it is right to kill it. See Klusendorf, *The Case for Life* (Wheaton, IL: Crossway, 2009), 173.

5. David C. Reardon, *Aborted Women, Silent No More* (Chicago: Loyola University Press, 1987), 206.

6. Researcher David Reardon concluded, "As with other 'psychological indications for abortion,' the evidence actually shows that rape is a strong contraindication for abortion." (Reardon, *Aborted Women, Silent No More,* 192.)

Why this is so becomes clear when the trauma of rape is understood. As Dr. Reardon explains, "Victims of rape feel dirty, guilty, sexually violated, of low self-esteem, angry, fearful or hateful toward men. She may experience sexual dysfunction, she may feel she has lost control of her life. Now let's look at the symptoms of abortion. The woman feels dirty, guilty, sexually violated, of low self-esteem, angry, fearful or hateful toward men. She may experience sexual dysfunction, she may feel she has lost control of her life. All the same symptoms. Some women have described the abortion experience as feeling like rape—a form of surgical rape. Abortion then is a 'cure' that only aggravates the problem." ("The Abortion Experience for Victims of Rape and Incest," *Association for Interdisciplinary Research Newsletter,* 2, no. 1 [Fall 1988], 4–6).

Incest victims face the same dilemma. People uncomfortable with or unwilling to address the special needs of a woman in this situation offer abortion as the only solution, masking their own discomfort in dealing with the trauma. Ultimately, abortion serves the selfish interests of the incestuous relative/perpetrator—namely, by destroying the unborn child who is tangible evidence of his evil acts. Edith Young was a rape and incest victim at age twelve. She writes, "I was being sexually attacked, threatened by him and betrayed by Mom's silence . . . The abortion which was to be in 'my best interest' has not been . . . it only saved their reputations, solved their problems and allowed their lives to go merrily on." (*Aborted Women, Silent No More*, 217.)

Abortion is to an incestuous male what a getaway car is to a bank robber: part of the escape plan. In 1990, a Baltimore court sentenced a man to 30 years in prison for raping his three daughters over a nine-year period. During the trial, it was revealed that the continual rape of these three girls resulted in ten pregnancies and ten abortions. How much better would it have been if the first pregnancy had continued. The incestuous father would have been exposed and sent to jail nine years earlier. The first victim would have been spared from ongoing sexual assault and her sisters would have been spared altogether.

7. See Makimaa, Sobie, Reardon, *Victims and Victors* (Springfield, IL: Acorn Books, 2000). Reardon's study found a 73 percent birthrate among the 164 pregnant rape victims he interviewed.

8. David Reardon, "Rape, Incest and Abortion: Searching Beyond the Myths," http://afterabortion.org/2004/rape-incest-and-abortion-searching-beyond-the-myths-3/.

9. What about abortion to "save the life" of the mother? The vast majority of abortions worldwide are not medically necessary to save the mother's physical life. They are done to delay giving birth or for socioeconomic concerns that include "disruption of education or

employment; lack of support from the father; desire to provide schooling for existing children; and poverty, unemployment or inability to afford additional children." See Akinrinola Bankole, Susheela Singh and Taylor Haas, "Reasons Why Women Have Induced Abortions: Evidence from 27 Countries," *International Family Planning Perspectives* 24, no. 3, September 1998.

But there are medical conditions, such as an ectopic pregnancy (EP) that is life threatening. Scott Klusendorf explains, "Pro-life advocates do not say that it's always wrong to take human life. Rather, we say it is always wrong to intentionally kill innocent human beings, and we believe elective abortion does just that . . . There is no way the developing human can survive EP. If the mother dies from internal bleeding, the embryo dies also, given he's too young to survive on his own. At the same time, the limits of current medical technology do not allow transfer to a more suitable environment. Despite our best intentions, we simply can't save the child.

What is the greatest moral good we can achieve in this situation? Is it best to do nothing and let two humans (likely) die or is it best to act in such a way that we save one life even though the unintended and unavoidable consequence of acting is the death of the human embryo? Pro-life advocates almost universally agree we should do the latter." (John Ensor and Scott Klusendorff, *Students for Life [Peabody, MA: Hendrickson, 2012]*, 82–83.)

10. These words are attributed to Martin Luther. But no one has been able to document where.

11. Eva Fogalman, *Conscience and Courage: Rescuers of Jews During the Holocaust* (New York: Anchor Books, 1994), 70.

12. Corrie ten Boom, *The Hiding Place* (New York: Bantam Books, 1974), 99.

Chapter 8: Our Heritage and Legacy

1. George Grant, *Third Time Around: A History of the Pro-Life Movement from the First Century to the Present* (Brentwood, TN: Wolgemuth & Hyatt, 1991), 12.

2. Clayton Jefford, ed., *The Didache in Context, Essays on Its Text, History and Transmission* (Leiden, The Netherlands: E.J. Brill, 1995), 1.1; 2.2.

3. Augustine, *On Marriage and Concupiscence* 1:17.15.

4. Susan B. Anthony, *The Revolution* (New York: July 8, 1869), 1,4,4.

5. David Reardon, *Aborted Women, Silent No More* (Chicago: Loyola University Press, 1987), 31.

6. Frederica Mathewes-Green, *Real Choices: Offering Practical, Life-Affirming Alternatives to Abortion* (Sisters, OR: Multnomah, 1994), 248.

7. Reardon, *Aborted Women, Silent No More,* 11.

8. Reardon, *Aborted Women, Silent No More,* 11.

9. P. G. Ney, T. Fung, A. R. Wickett, and C. Beaman-Dodd, "The Effects of Pregnancy Loss on Women's Health," *Journal of Science and Medicine* 38 (1994), 1193–1200.

10. Grant, *Third Time Around,* 20.

11. Emperor Valentinian, *The Code of Justinian* 8.52.2.

12. Grant, *Third Time Around,* 21. The *sagae,* Latin for "sorceress," is Grant's characterization of the women who traded on the fears of pregnant women by selling abortion services.

13. The same is true today. A man and woman can kill their baby through abortion. Yet if the unborn baby is killed in a car accident by a drunk driver, the driver can be charged with fetal homicide.

14. Grant, *Third Time Around*, 38.

15. For more on adoption, I recommend, Russell D. Moore, *Adopted for Life: The Priority of Adoption for Christian Families and Churches* (Wheaton, IL: Crossway, 2009).

16. We worked with licensed local adoption agencies or with Bethany Christian Services, a nationwide Christian adoption ministry (see www.Bethany.org).

17. Based on numbers reported by the Guttmacher Institute 1973–2008, with estimates of 1,212,400 for 2009–2012. GI estimates a possible 3% underreporting rate, which is factored into the total. Taken from the National Right to Life: http://www.nrlc.org/Factsheets/FS03_AbortionInTheUS.pdf.

18. John Calvin, *Calvin's Commentaries*, trans. Charles Bingham (Grand Rapids: Baker Book House, 1981), 3:42.

19. John Calvin, "Bearing the Cross, A Part of Self-Denial," in *The Institutes of the Christian Religion in 2 Vol.*, ed. John T McNeil, in The Library of Christian Classics, vol. 20 (Philadelphia: Westminster, 1977), 707.

20. Lambert Collier, *The Jesuits: The Warrior Priests of the Pope* (New York: Maethan Brothers, 1926), 87.

21. Grant, *Third Time Around*, 53.

22. Vishal and Ruth Mangalwadi, *The Legacy of William Carey: A Model for the Transformation of a Culture* (Wheaton, IL: Crossway, 1993), 17–25.

23. Cited in Timothy George, *Faithful Witness: the Life and Mission of William Carey* (Birmingham, AL: New Hope, 1991), 149.

24. Mangalwadi and Mangalwadi, *The Legacy of William Carey*, 33.

25. Grant, *Third Time Around*, 86.

26. Ruth Tucker, *From Jerusalem to Irian Jaya* (Grand Rapids: Zondervan, 1983), 240.

27. Elisabeth Elliot, *Amy Carmichael* (Grand Rapids: Zondervan, 1983), 169.

28. Tucker, *From Jerusalem to Irian Jaya*, 241.

29. For more information on Heartbeat International, see www.heartbeatinternational.org. For more information on Carenet, see www.care-net.org.

30. See http://abortiondocs.org/mission/.

31. Quoted in Charles Colson, *Kingdoms in Conflict* (Grand Rapids: Zondervan, 1987), 101.

32. To read Norma McCorvey's story in her own words, see *Won by Love: Norma McCorvey, Jane Roe of Roe v. Wade, Speaks Out for the Unborn as She Shares Her New Conviction for Life* (Nashville: Thomas Nelson, 1997).

33. Colson, *Kingdoms in Conflict*, 102.

Chapter 10: Final Encouragements

1. I developed this more in *Innocent Blood: Challenging the Powers of Death with the Gospel of Life* (Adelphi, MD: Cruciform Press, 2011), 59–70.

2. If you are interested in how I communicate this vision for abstinence till marriage and faithfulness within marriage, see John Ensor, *Doing Things Right in Matters of the Heart* (Wheaton, IL: Crossway, 2007).

3. Scott Klusendorf writes about "Co-Belligerence without Theological Compromise" in *The Case for Life* (Wheaton, IL: Crossway, 2009), 225–230.

4. Charles Swindoll, *The Sanctity of Life* (Dallas: Word, 1990), xiv.

5. I can be contacted at www.JohnEnsor.com.